WORKBOOK

3
FOCUS
ON
GRAMMAR
AN INTEGRATED SKILLS APPROACH

THIRD EDITION

MARJORIE FUCHS

PEARSON
Longman

FOCUS ON GRAMMAR 3: An Integrated Skills Approach
Workbook

Pearson Education, 10 Bank Street, White Plains, NY 10606

Staff credits: The people who made up the **Focus on Grammar 3 Workbook** team, representing editorial, production, design, and manufacturing, are listed below: Rhea Banker, Nancy Blodgett, Aerin Csigay, Karen Davy, Christine Edmonds, Nancy Flaggman, Ann France, Laura Le Dréan, and Kathleen Silloway.
Cover images: (center) Harold Sund/Getty Images, (middle) Nick Koudis/Getty Images, (background) Comstock Images/Getty Images
Text composition: ElectraGraphics, Inc.
Text font: 11/13 Sabon, 10/13 Myriad Roman
Illustrator: Susan Scott, pp. 25, 170, 171.
Photo credits: **p. 5** *(left)* Digital Vision/Getty Images, *(right)* Amos Morgan/Getty Images; **p. 15** *(top)* Bettmann/Corbis, *(bottom)* Bettmann/Corbis; **p. 16** Library of Congress; **p. 18** AP/Wide World Photos; **p. 56** Trapper Frank/Corbis Sygma; **p. 78** *(top)* Allsport Photography USA, Inc., *(bottom)* Reuters/Corbis; **p. 92** RubberBall Productions; **p. 95** Hulton Getty; **p. 106** Image Source/Getty Images; **p. 114** Royalty-Free/Corbis; **p. 118** Colin Garratt/Milepost $92^1/2$/Corbis; **p. 135** RubberBall Productions.

ISBN: 0-13-189990-2 (Workbook)

LONGMAN ON THE **WEB**

Longman.com offers online resources for teachers and students. Access our Companion Websites, our online catalog, and our local offices around the world.

Visit us at **longman.com.**

Printed in the United States of America
10 V001 12 11 10

Contents

PART VI: Adjectives and Adverbs

PART VII: Gerunds and Infinitives

PART VIII: More Modals and Similar Expressions

About the Author

Marjorie Fuchs has taught ESL at New York City Technical College and LaGuardia Community College of the City University of New York and EFL at the Sprach Studio Lingua Nova in Munich, Germany. She holds a master's degree in Applied English Linguistics and a Certificate in TESOL from the University of Wisconsin–Madison. She has authored and co-authored many widely used books and multimedia materials, notably **Crossroads, Top Twenty ESL Word Games: Beginning Vocabulary Development, Families: Ten Card Games for Language Learners, Focus on Grammar 3** and **4: An Integrated Skills Approach, Focus on Grammar 3** and **4 CD-ROM, Longman English Interactive 3** and **4, Grammar Express Basic, Grammar Express Basic CD-ROM, Grammar Express Intermediate,** and the workbooks to the **Longman Dictionary of American English,** the **Longman Photo Dictionary, The Oxford Picture Dictionary, Focus on Grammar 3,** and **Grammar Express Basic.**

Present Progressive and Simple Present

1 | SPELLING

Write the correct forms of the verbs. Make spelling changes where necessary.

	-ing	*-s* or *-es*
1. do	doing	does
2. get	_____	_____
3. give	_____	_____
4. grab	_____	_____
5. have	_____	_____
6. plan	_____	_____
7. say	_____	_____
8. start	_____	_____
9. try	_____	_____
10. watch	_____	_____

2 | PRESENT PROGRESSIVE OR SIMPLE PRESENT

Read the sentences about a student, Antonio Lopes. Complete the sentences. Use the present progressive or the simple present form of the verbs in parentheses. Use contractions when possible.

1. It's 8:00 A.M. Antonio Lopes _____*is driving*_____ to school.
  (drive)
2. He _____ to school every day.
  (drive)
3. The trip usually _____ 25 minutes.
  (take)
4. Today it _____ 25 minutes.
  (not take)
5. It _____ much longer.
  (take)

(continued)

6. Workers _____ the highway this morning.
   (repair)

7. Because of the construction, Antonio _____ Parson Road.
   (use)

8. He _____ usually _____ Parson Road.
   (not use)

9. Normally, he _____ Route 93.
   (take)

10. Traffic always _____ faster on Route 93.
    (move)

11. Today, the weather _____ the traffic too.
    (slow down)

12. It _____ hard, and the roads are slippery.
    (rain)

13. Antonio _____ to drive in the rain.
    (not like)

14. He always _____ slowly when the roads are wet.
    (drive)

15. The radio is on, and Antonio _____ to the traffic report.
    (listen)

16. He always _____ to the radio on his way to school.
    (listen)

17. The announcer _____ an accident on Parson Road.
    (describe)

18. Traffic _____ because of the accident.
    (not move)

19. Antonio _____ to drive when the traffic is bad.
    (hate)

20. He _____ to be late for school.
    (not want)

21. He never _____ relaxed when he is behind the wheel.
    (feel)

22. He _____ he can't do anything about the traffic conditions.
    (know)

23. Antonio _____ sorry he didn't take the bus instead!
    (be)

3 | PERSONALIZATION

Complete these statements with information about yourself. Use the present progressive or the simple present.

1. At the moment, _____.

2. I always _____.

3. I never _____.

4. These days _____.

5. I sometimes _____, but now I _____.

4 | PRESENT PROGRESSIVE OR SIMPLE PRESENT

Complete the following postcards with the present progressive or simple present form of the verbs in the boxes. Use contractions when possible.

| get | have | look | rain | stand | start | take | ~~travel~~ |

A.

Dear Carlos,

Ana and I _____are traveling_____ through England. Right now I
        1.

_____ in front of Big Ben. It's a cloudy day. The sky
   2.

_____ darker by the minute. It _____ like it's going to
   3.   **4.**

rain. (It _____ here a lot!) Ana _____ her camera, and
       5.   **6.**

she _____ pictures. Oh, no! It _____ to rain.
   7.   **8.**

See you in a few weeks!

Marcos

| help | improve | live | love | miss | speak | study | want |

B.

Dear Amanda,

    Here I am in Paris! I _____ it here. It's a
                     1.

beautiful city. I _____ French and _____
         2.   **3.**

with a French family—the Michauds. My French _____ because I
                     4.

always _____ it "at home."
      5.

    The Michauds are great. They _____ me find a job. I
                     6.

_____ to save enough money to travel in August. Why don't you
  7.

come and visit me? I _____ you!
                 8.

              Melissa

5 | AFFIRMATIVE STATEMENTS

Aldo and Emilia Bottero are students. Look at what they do every day. Complete the sentences about their activities. Choose between the present progressive and the simple present.

Aldo	
A.M.	
7:30	get up
8:00	read the newspaper
8:30	go to school
P.M.	
12:00	have lunch
1:00	work at the bookstore
4:00	play soccer
5:00	go home
6:00	have dinner
7:00	do homework
8:00	play computer games

Emilia	
A.M.	
7:30	get up
8:00	run
8:30	go to school
P.M.	
12:00	have lunch
1:00	study at the library
4:00	play basketball
5:00	do homework at the library
6:00	practice the guitar
7:00	have dinner
8:00	watch TV

1. At 7:30 A.M., *Aldo and Emilia get up.* _____

2. It's 8:00 A.M. *Aldo is reading the newspaper. Emilia is running.* _____

3. At 8:30 A.M., _____

4. It's noon. _____

5. At 1:00 P.M., _____

6. At 4:00 P.M., _____

7. It's 5:00 P.M. _____

8. At 6:00 P.M., _____

9. At 7:00 P.M., _____

10. It's 8:00 P.M. _____

6 | AFFIRMATIVE AND NEGATIVE STATEMENTS

Read this article about Aldo and Emilia from the school newsletter. There are five mistakes in facts about their schedules. Look at their schedules in Exercise 5. Then correct the mistakes.

Modern Language Institute Newsletter

Welcome, New Students!

We are happy to welcome two new students, Aldo and Emilia Bottero from Rome, Italy. The Botteros have a very busy schedule. They both get up at 8:30 every morning. Then Aldo watches TV, and Emilia goes for her morning run. They then leave for the Institute where they are studying English this summer. After three hours of class, they have lunch together. After lunch, Emilia works at the bookstore. Both students love all types of sports. These days Aldo is playing soccer and Emilia is playing tennis. Emilia also plays the guitar. "We're very happy to be here," they said. "Our days are busy, but we always have dinner together. Just like back home in Italy."

1. _They don't get up at 8:30._

    They get up at 7:30.

2. _____

    _____

3. _____

    _____

4. _____

    _____

5. _____

    _____

7 | QUESTIONS AND SHORT ANSWERS

Use the words in parentheses and the present progressive or simple present to write questions about Aldo and Emilia. Look at their schedules in Exercise 5 and answer the questions.

1. (Aldo and Emilia / go to school)

   A: *Do Aldo and Emilia go to school?*

   B: *Yes, they do.*

2. (When / Aldo and Emilia / get up)

   A: _____

   B: _____

3. (Emilia / walk in the morning)

   A: _____

   B: _____

4. It's 12:00. (What / they / do / now)

   A: _____

   B: _____

5. It's 1:00. (Aldo / do homework now)

   A: _____

   B: _____

6. (Emilia / do her homework at school)

   A: _____

   B: _____

7. (When / Emilia / play basketball)

   A: _____

   B: _____

8. (Aldo / play computer games before dinner)

   A: _____

   B: _____

8 | ADVERBS AND WORD ORDER

Unscramble the words to make sentences. Use the correct form of the verbs in parentheses.

1. Aldo / the newspaper / (read) / always

   *Aldo always reads the newspaper.*_____

2. on time / usually / Emilia / (be)

   _____

3. never / school / Aldo and Emilia / (miss)

   _____

4. these days / they / (study) / English

   _____

5. usually / they / Italian / (speak)

   _____

6. (speak) / English / now / they

   _____

7. (do) / their homework / Aldo and Emilia / always

   _____

8. (be) / Aldo / tired / often

   _____

9. usually / (eat) / the students / in school / lunch

   _____

10. hungry / they / (be) / always

    _____

11. Emilia / at the moment / (have) / a snack

    _____

12. (go) / to bed / rarely / Emilia / late

    _____

9 | EDITING

Read this student's e-mail. There are eleven mistakes in the use of the present progressive or simple present. The first mistake is already corrected. Find and correct ten more.

Hi, Andrew!

How are you? ~~I write~~ *I'm writing* you this e-mail before my class.

I am having a part-time job as a clerk in the mail room of a small company. The pay isn't good, but I'm liking the people there. They're all friendly, and we are speaking Spanish all the time. I'm also taking Spanish classes at night at a language institute. The class is meeting three times a week. It just started last week, so I'm not knowing many of the other students yet. They seem nice, though.

I'm thinking that I'm beginning to get accustomed to living here. At first I experienced some "culture shock." I understand that this is quite normal. But these days I meet more and more people because of my job and my class, so I'm feeling more connected to things.

What do you do these days? Do you still look for a new job?

Please write when you can. I'm always liking to hear from you.

Brian

10 | PERSONALIZATION

Write a note to a friend. Tell your friend what you are doing these days.

_____

_____

_____

_____

_____

_____

_____

_____

Imperative

1 | AFFIRMATIVE AND NEGATIVE IMPERATIVES

Write affirmative and negative imperatives with the words in the box. Change the underlined words.

backward	bottom	~~down~~	in	late	~~left~~	light	loudly
low	off	shut	slowly	small	tight	up	white

Affirmative

Negative

1. Bend your <u>right</u> leg.

   Don't bend your left leg.

2. *Look down.*

Don't look <u>up</u>.

3. Lean <u>forward</u>.

4. _____

Don't take a <u>big</u> step.

5. Breathe <u>out</u>.

6. _____

Don't count <u>quickly</u>.

7. Speak <u>softly</u>.

8. _____

Don't keep your eyes <u>open</u>.

9. Wear <u>loose</u> clothes.

10. _____

Don't wear a <u>black</u> T-shirt.

11. _____

Don't wear <u>heavy</u> clothes.

12. Turn the lights <u>on</u>.

13. _____

Don't turn the music <u>down</u>.

14. _____

Don't put the heat on <u>high</u>.

15. Come <u>early</u>.

16. Lock the <u>top</u> lock.

2 | AFFIRMATIVE AND NEGATIVE IMPERATIVES

Ada, a student, is asking her friends for directions to Jim's Gym. Look at the map and complete the conversation. Use the affirmative or negative imperative form of the verbs in the box.

~~ask~~	be	continue	cross	give	go	have	make
pass	ride	show	stop	~~take~~	turn	walk	work

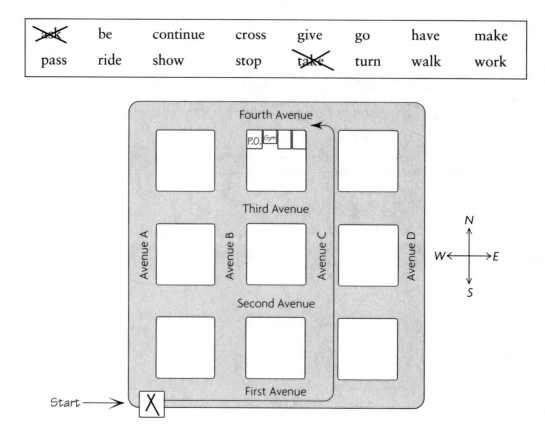

ADA: Hi, guys. How are you doing?

BOB: Hey, Ada. What's up?

ADA: I'm going to take an exercise class at Jim's Gym. Do you know how to get there?

BOB: Jim's Gym? _____Ask_____ Chen. He's taking a class there.
     1.

ADA: I didn't know that. Which bus do you take to the gym, Chen?

CHEN: Oh, _____don't take_____ the bus! It's not far from here.
        2.

_____ or _____ your bike. It's good exercise!
      3.   4.

ADA: I'll walk. How do I get there? _____ me on this map, OK?
                                              5.

CHEN: Sure. _____ me the map and I'll show you. _____ two blocks
              6.   7.

east on First Avenue.

ADA: East? You mean turn left?

CHEN: No. _____ left. Go right when you leave the building. OK? Then
　　　　　　　　8.

_____ a left turn when you get to Avenue C. _____ on Avenue
　　9.　　　　　　　　　　　　　　　　　　　　　　　　　　　　　　　10.

C, but _____ when you reach Fourth Avenue. _____ Fourth
　　　　　　11.　　　　　　　　　　　　　　　　　　　　　　　　　12.

Avenue. It's another left at Fourth. But _____ careful. Jim's Gym is small,
　　　　　　　　　　　　　　　　　　　　　13.

and it's easy to miss. _____ the post office. The gym is right before it.
　　　　　　　　　　　14.

ADA: Thanks.

CHEN: Sure. _____ fun! _____ too hard!
　　　　　　　15.　　　　　　　　　16.

3 | EDITING

Read Ada's note to her roommate. There are six mistakes in the use of imperatives. The first mistake is already corrected. Find and correct five more.

> Sarah
>
> 　　　　　　　　　　　　　*Call*
> Your mother called. ~~Calls~~ her at your sister's tonight.
>
> Don't call after 10:00, though.
>
> I went to the gym.
>
> Wash please the dishes and threw out the trash.
>
> If anyone calls for me, takes a message.
>
> Thanks a lot and has a good evening!
>
> A.

4 | PERSONALIZATION

Draw a map and give directions to a place near you. Use your own paper.

3 Simple Past

1 | SPELLING: REGULAR AND IRREGULAR VERBS

Write the simple past form of the verbs.

Base Form	Simple Past	Base Form	Simple Past
1. answer	answered	16. look	_____
2. begin	_____	17. meet	_____
3. buy	_____	18. move	_____
4. catch	_____	19. need	_____
5. come	_____	20. open	_____
6. die	_____	21. put	_____
7. do	_____	22. read	_____
8. feel	_____	23. say	_____
9. find	_____	24. see	_____
10. get	_____	25. take	_____
11. give	_____	26. think	_____
12. have	_____	27. understand	_____
13. hurry	_____	28. vote	_____
14. kiss	_____	29. win	_____
15. live	_____	30. write	_____

31. The past of *be* is _____ or _____.

2 | AFFIRMATIVE AND NEGATIVE STATEMENTS: *BE*

Look at the chart of famous writers of the past. Complete the sentences with **was**, **wasn't**, **were**, *and* **weren't**.

ISAAK BABEL	1894–1941	Russia	short-story writer, playwright*
SIMONE DE BEAUVOIR	1908–1966	France	novelist,** essayist***
GIOVANNI BOCCACCIO	1313–1375	Italy	poet, storyteller
KAREL ČAPEK	1890–1938	Czechoslovakia	novelist, essayist
AGATHA CHRISTIE	1890–1976	England	mystery writer
LORRAINE HANSBERRY	1930–1965	United States	playwright
NAZIM HIKMET	1902–1963	Turkey	poet, playwright, novelist
LUCY M. MONTGOMERY	1874–1942	Canada	poet, novelist
PABLO NERUDA	1904–1973	Chile	poet

> * A *playwright* writes plays.
> ** A *novelist* writes novels (books that are fiction).
> *** An *essayist* writes essays (short pieces of writing about a topic).

1. Simone de Beauvoir _____*wasn't*_____ a French poet.

   She _____*was*_____ a French novelist.

2. Giovanni Boccaccio _____ born in 1313.

3. Lucy M. Montgomery and Lorraine Hansberry _____ South American writers.

   They _____ North American writers.

4. Karel Čapek _____ a poet.

5. Pablo Neruda _____ from Chile.

6. Agatha Christie _____ American.

   She _____ British.

7. Isaak Babel _____ Russian.

   He _____ French.

8. Nazim Hikmet _____ from Russia.

   He _____ from Turkey.

9. Babel and Hikmet _____ both playwrights.

10. Pablo Neruda and Simone de Beauvoir _____ both born in the early 1900s.

3 | QUESTIONS AND ANSWERS WITH THE PAST OF *BE*

Use **was** *and* **wasn't** *and the words in parentheses to write questions about the writers in Exercise 2. Look at the chart in Exercise 2 and answer the questions.*

1. (Lorraine Hansberry / a playwright)

   A: *Was Lorraine Hansberry a playwright?*

   B: *Yes, she was.*

2. (Where / Simone de Beauvoir from)

   A: _____

   B: _____

3. (What nationality / Pablo Neruda)

   A: _____

   B: _____

4. (Who / Boccaccio)

   A: _____

   B: _____

5. (Agatha Christie / French)

   A: _____

   B: _____

6. (What nationality / Lucy M. Montgomery)

   A: _____

   B: _____

7. (Nazim Hikmet / a poet)

   A: _____

   B: _____

8. (When / Karel Čapek / born)

   A: _____

   B: _____

9. (Who / Isaak Babel)

   A: _____

   B: _____

4 | AFFIRMATIVE STATEMENTS

Complete the following short biographies with the simple past form of the verbs in the boxes.

| ~~be~~ | begin | die | grow up | love | move | teach | use | write |

A.

Béla Bartók (1881–1945) _____*was*_____ one of the most famous
1.
composers of the 20th century. Born in Hungary, he _____
2.
in a musical family. His mother _____ him how to play
3.
the piano, and at the age of nine he _____ to write music.
4.
Bartók _____ the folk music of his native country. He
5.
_____ these folk tunes, and folk music from other Eastern
6.
European countries, in his own work. In addition to his compositions for musical instruments, he

also _____ an opera and a ballet. Bartók _____ to the United States
7.   8.
in 1940 and _____ there at the age of 64.
9.

| be | begin | die | have | love | marry | paint | plan | study | teach |

B.

Frida Kahlo (1907–1954) _____ one of the most famous
1.
Mexican painters. At first she _____ to be a doctor, but after
2.
a serious accident she _____ painting pictures of her family
3.
and friends from her bed. She also _____ pictures
4.
of herself. Kahlo never _____ art in school. She
5.
_____ herself how to paint, and people _____
6.   7.
her work. In 1929 she _____ Diego Rivera, another very famous Mexican painter.
8.
Unfortunately, Kahlo _____ a lot of serious medical problems, and she
9.
_____ at the age of 47.
10.

(continued)

be	build	fly	last	take place	watch

C.

Orville Wright (1871–1948) and **Wilbur Wright** (1867–1912)

_____ **1.** American airplane inventors. The two brothers

_____ **2.** their first planes in their bicycle shop in Ohio.

On December 17, 1903, Orville _____ **3.** their plane,

Flyer 1, a distance of 120 feet. Wilbur, four other men, and a boy

_____ **4.** from the ground below. This first controlled, power-driven flight

_____ **5.** near Kitty Hawk, North Carolina. It _____ **6.** only about

12 seconds.

---

5 | QUESTIONS AND ANSWERS

Use the words in parentheses and the simple past to write questions about the people in Exercise 4. Look at the information in Exercise 4 and answer the questions.

Biography A

1. (When / Béla Bartók / live)

   A: *When did Béla Bartók live?*

   B: *He lived from 1881 to 1945.*

2. (Where / he / grow up)

   A: _____

   B: _____

3. (What / he / do)

   A: _____

   B: _____

4. (he / spend / his whole life in Hungary)

   A: _____

   B: _____

Biography B

5. (Frida Kahlo / plan to be a painter)

   A: _____

   B: _____

6. (When / she / begin painting)

   A: _____

   B: _____

7. (What / she / paint)

   A: _____

   B: _____

8. (When / she / die)

   A: _____

   B: _____

Biography C

9. (Where / the Wright brothers / build their first planes)

   A: _____

   B: _____

10. (both brothers / fly the *Flyer 1*)

    A: _____

    B: _____

11. (Where / the first controlled flight / take place)

    A: _____

    B: _____

12. (How long / the flight / last)

    A: _____

    B: _____

6 | NEGATIVE STATEMENTS

There were a lot of similarities between the Wright brothers, but there were also differences. Complete the chart about the differences between Orville and Wilbur.

Orville	**Wilbur**
1. Orville talked a lot.	*Wilbur didn't talk a lot.*
2. *Orville didn't spend a lot of time alone.*	Wilbur spent a lot of time alone.
3. _____	Wilbur had serious health problems.
4. Orville grew a moustache.	_____
5. _____	Wilbur lost most of his hair.
6. Orville took courses in Latin.	_____
7. Orville liked to play jokes.	_____
8. Orville dressed very fashionably.	_____
9. Orville played the guitar.	_____
10. _____	Wilbur built the first glider.
11. _____	Wilbur made the first attempts to fly.
12. _____	Wilbur chose the location of Kitty Hawk.
13. Orville had a lot of patience.	_____
14. Orville lived a long life.	_____

7 | EDITING

Read this student's short biography of a famous person. There are six mistakes in the use of the simple past. The first mistake is already corrected. Find and correct five more.

       Pablo Neruda (1904–1973) ~~were~~ *was* a famous poet, political activist, and diplomat. He was born in Parral, Chile. When he was 17, he gone to Santiago to continue his education. He did not finished, but he soon published his first book. Neruda spends the next several decades traveling and continuing to write poetry. In 1971, while he was Chile's ambassador to France, he winned the Nobel Prize in literature. He dead two years later.

Past Progressive and Simple Past

1 | AFFIRMATIVE AND NEGATIVE STATEMENTS WITH THE PAST PROGRESSIVE

Frank Cotter is a financial manager. Read his schedule. Use the affirmative or negative past progressive to complete the sentences.

April 10	
Wednesday	
9:00–10:00	meet with Ms. Jacobs
10:00–11:00	write financial reports
11:00–12:00	answer correspondence
12:00–1:00	eat lunch with Mr. Webb at Sol's Cafe
1:00–3:00	attend lecture at City University
3:00–4:00	discuss budget with Alan
4:00–5:00	return phone calls

1. At 9:30, Mr. Cotter _____*was meeting*_____ with Ms. Jacobs.

2. At 9:30, he _____ financial reports.

3. At 11:30, he _____ correspondence.

4. At 12:30, he and Mr. Webb _____ lunch.

(continued)

5. They _____ at Frank's Diner.

6. At 2:00, he _____ a lecture.

7. At 3:30, he and Alan _____ sales reports.

8. They _____ the budget.

9. At 4:30, he _____ correspondence.

10. He _____ phone calls.

2 | QUESTIONS AND ANSWERS WITH THE PAST PROGRESSIVE

Use the words in parentheses to write questions. Look at the schedule in Exercise 1 and write the answers. Use the past progressive.

1. (Mr. Cotter / meet / with Mr. Webb at 9:30)

   A: *Was Mr. Cotter meeting with Mr. Webb at 9:30?*

   B: *No, he wasn't.*

2. (What / he / do at 9:30)

   A: _____

   B: _____

3. (Mr. Cotter / write police reports at 10:30)

   A: _____

   B: _____

4. (What kind of reports / he / write)

   A: _____

   B: _____

5. (What / he / do at 11:30)

   A: _____

   B: _____

6. (he / have lunch at 12:00)

   A: _____

   B: _____

7. (Who / eat lunch with him)

   A: _____

   B: _____

8. (Where / they / have lunch)

   A: _____

   B: _____

9. (Who / he / talk to at 3:30)

   A: _____

   B: _____

10. (What / they / discuss)

   A: _____

   B: _____

3 | STATEMENTS WITH THE PAST PROGRESSIVE AND SIMPLE PAST

Read this newspaper article. Complete the story with the past progressive or simple past form of the verbs in parentheses.

HIT AND RUN

   Last Friday at 5:30 P.M., a blue Honda Accord _____*hit*_____ 35-year-old Lisa
                                                  1. (hit)

Coleman while she _____ the street at Broadway and 10th Avenue.
                   2. (cross)

Witnesses say that the car _____ and _____ at the red light.
                           3. (speed)   **4. (not stop)**

   Frank Cotter, a financial manager at Smith Webber, _____ on his way
                                                       5. (be)

home from work when he _____ the accident. "I _____ along
                       6. (see)   **7. (walk)**

Broadway when I _____ this blue Honda. I _____ it because
                8. (see)   **9. (notice)**

it _____ very fast. When it _____ the intersection, the driver
   10. (go)   **11. (reach)**

_____ right through the red light. Seconds later, the car _____
12. (go)   **13. (hit)**

the pedestrian. I immediately _____ my cell phone and _____
                              14. (take out)   **15. (call)**

the police. The driver _____."
                       16. (not stop)

(continued)

The accident _____ just a few blocks from General Hospital, and the
17. (happen)

ambulance _____ quickly. When it _____ to the scene of the
18. (come)   **19. (get)**

accident, Coleman _____ on the ground. She _____ from a
20. (lie)   **21. (bleed)**

head wound, but she _____ conscious and the police _____
22. (be)   **23. (question)**

her about the accident.

Coleman _____ that she _____ the street when the car
24. (say)   **25. (cross)**

_____ through the light and _____ her down. "It all
26. (go)   **27. (knock)**

_____ so quickly," she said. "I _____ a green light, and I
28. (happen)   **29. (have)**

_____ the street when all of a sudden—boom! I _____ the car."
30. (cross)   **31. (not see)**

Coleman _____ her arm and _____ some injuries to her
32. (break)   **33. (have)**

head, but fortunately, they _____ very serious. Police are still looking for the
34. (not be)

driver of the Honda.

---

4 | QUESTIONS WITH THE PAST PROGRESSIVE AND SIMPLE PAST

*The police are interviewing another witness to the accident. Use the words in parentheses
and the past progressive or simple past to write the interview questions.*

1. (What / you / do / when the accident / happen)

    OFFICER: *What were you doing when the accident happened?*

    WITNESS: I was riding my bike home from school when I heard a loud noise.

2. (What / you / do / when you / hear the noise)

    OFFICER: _____

    WITNESS: I got off my bike and looked in the direction of the sound.

3. (What / you / see / when you / look in the direction of the sound)

    OFFICER: _____

    WITNESS: I saw a car—a blue Honda.

4. (Where / you / stand / when you / see the Honda)

    OFFICER: _____

    WITNESS: I was at the corner of Broadway and 10th.

5. (the driver / stop / when the accident / occur)

OFFICER: _____

WITNESS: No. The driver didn't stop.

6. (What / happen / next)

OFFICER: _____

WITNESS: I tried to get the license plate number, but the car was moving too fast.

7. (you / get a look at the driver / while he / drive away)

OFFICER: _____

WITNESS: No, I didn't. I don't even know if it was a man or a woman.

8. (What / the victim / do / when the car / hit her)

OFFICER: _____

WITNESS: I don't know. I didn't see her before the car hit her.

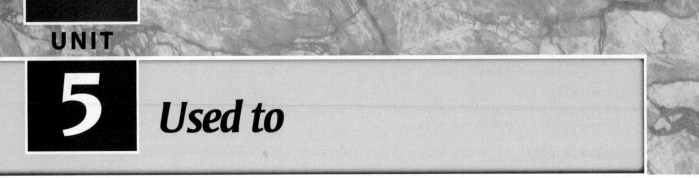

1 | AFFIRMATIVE STATEMENTS

Life in many countries isn't the way it used to be. Complete the chart.

In the Past	Now
1. <u> People used to ride </u> horses.	People ride in cars.
2. _____ by candlelight.	People read by electric light.
3. _____ over open fires.	People cook in microwave ovens.
4. _____ all of their clothes by hand.	People wash most of their clothes in washing machines.
5. _____ manual typewriters.	People use word processors and computers.
6. _____ weeks to get a message to another country.	It takes just a few seconds.

2 | AFFIRMATIVE AND NEGATIVE STATEMENTS

Read the sentences about the assistant manager of a California bank, Yoko Shimizu.
Complete the sentences with the correct form of **used to** *and the verbs in parentheses.*

1. Yoko _____<u>used to be</u>_____ a full-time student. Now she has a job at a bank.
                 (be)

2. She _____ with a computer. Now she uses one every day.
            (work)

3. She _____ a car. Now she owns a 2004 Toyota Corolla.
            (have)

4. Yoko _____ the bus to work. Now she drives.
            (take)

5. The bus _____ crowded. These days it's hard to find a seat.
            (be)

6. Yoko _____ in New York. Then she moved to Los Angeles.
            (live)

7. She _____ Los Angeles. Now she thinks it's a nice city.
            (like)

8. She _____ a lot of people in Los Angeles. Now she has a lot of
   (know)
   friends there.

9. She _____ to New York several times a year. These days she doesn't
   (return)
   go there very often.

10. She _____ a lot of phone calls. Now she sends a lot of e-mails instead.
    (make)

3 | QUESTIONS AND ANSWERS

Use **used to** *and the words in parentheses to write questions about Lisa White. Look at the two ID cards to write the answers.*

1. (live in California)

   A: *Did she use to live in California?* _____

   B: *No, she didn't.* _____

2. Lisa recently moved to Los Angeles. (Where / live)

   A: _____

   B: _____

3. Lisa lives in a house. (live in a house)

   A: _____

   B: _____

4. This is her first job. (What / do)

   A: _____

   B: _____

(continued)

5. (Which school / attend)

A: _____

B: _____

6. Lisa looks very different from before. She has short hair. (have long hair)

A: _____

B: _____

7. (wear glasses)

A: _____

B: _____

8. Lisa's last name is different from before. (be married)

A: _____

B: _____

4 | EDITING

Read this student's journal entry. There are eight mistakes in the use of **used to**. The first mistake is already corrected. Find and correct seven more.

Sunday, Oct. 5

Today I ran into an old classmate. We used to be in the same science class. In fact, we used
to study
to ~~studied~~ together for tests. He was a very good student, and he always uses to get A's. At
first I almost didn't recognize Jason! He looked so different. He used to had very dark hair.
Now he's almost all gray. He also used to being a little heavy. Now he's quite thin. And he was
wearing a suit and tie! I couldn't believe it. He never use to dress that way. He only used to
wore jeans! His personality seemed different too. He didn't used to talk very much. Now he
seems very outgoing. I wonder what he thought of me! I'm sure I look and act different from
the way I was used to too!

5 | PERSONALIZATION

Write five sentences about how your life used to be different from the way it is now. Use
used to and **didn't use to**. Use your own paper.

Future

1 | AFFIRMATIVE STATEMENTS WITH *BE GOING TO*

Read the situations. Use the words in the box and a form of **be going to** *or*
not be going to *to write predictions or guesses.*

crash	eat lunch	get a ticket	get gas
make a left turn	rain	~~take a trip~~	wash the car

1. Professor Starr is carrying two suitcases toward his car.

   He's going to take a trip.

2. Ms. Marshall has a bucket of water, soap, and a sponge.

   _____

3. Mr. and Mrs. Johnson are driving into an Exxon service station.

   _____

4. Fred is driving behind a woman in a black sports car. Her left indicator light is flashing.

   _____

5. Tiffany is driving 70 miles per hour in a 50-mile-per-hour zone. A police officer is right behind her.

   _____

6. A blue Ford is driving directly toward a white Toyota. They don't have time to stop.

   _____

7. It's noon. The Smiths are driving into a Burger King parking lot.

   _____

8. The sky is full of dark clouds.

   _____

2 | QUESTIONS WITH *BE GOING TO*

*Use the words in parentheses to write questions. Use **be going to**.*

1. (What / you / do this summer)

   A: *What are you going to do this summer?*

   B: My wife and I are going to take a trip to San Francisco.

2. (How long / you / stay)

   A: _____

   B: Just for a week.

3. (you / stay at a hotel)

   A: _____

   B: Yes. We're staying at a hotel in North Beach.

4. (What / you / do in San Francisco)

   A: _____

   B: Oh, the usual, I suppose. Sightseeing and shopping.

5. (you / visit Fisherman's Wharf)

   A: _____

   B: Yes. We're going to take one of those city bus tours.

6. (your daughter / go with you)

   A: _____

   B: No, she's going to attend summer school. Our son isn't going either.

7. (What / he / do)

   A: _____

   B: He got a job at an Italian restaurant.

8. (When / you / leave)

   A: _____

   B: June 11.

   A: Have a good trip.

   B: Thanks.

3 | AFFIRMATIVE AND NEGATIVE STATEMENTS WITH *BE GOING TO*

Look at Professor and Mrs. Starr's boarding passes. Then read the sentences. All of them have incorrect information. Correct the information.

1. Professor Starr is going to go to Los Angeles.

   He isn't going to go to Los Angeles.

   He's going to go to San Francisco.

2. He's going to take the train.

   _____

   _____

3. He's going to travel alone.

   _____

   _____

4. The Starrs are going to leave from Chicago.

   _____

   _____

(continued)

5. They're going to fly US Airways.

_____

_____

6. They're going to leave on July 11.

_____

_____

7. They're going to take Flight 149.

_____

_____

8. The plane is going to depart at 7:00 A.M.

_____

_____

9. The Starrs are going to sit apart.

_____

_____

10. Mrs. Starr is going to sit in Seat 15B.

_____

_____

4 | AFFIRMATIVE AND NEGATIVE STATEMENTS, QUESTIONS, AND SHORT ANSWERS WITH *WILL*

Mrs. Starr is reading an interview about personal robots in the airplane magazine.
*Complete the interview with the verbs in parentheses and **will** or **won't**.*

INTERVIEWER: We all know that robots are already working in factories. But tell us something

about the future. _____*Will*_____ people _____*have*_____ robots at home?

1. (have)

SCIENTIST: They already do! There are, for example, small robots that vacuum the floor. I

believe that before too long, personal robots _____ as common in

2. (become)

the home as personal computers are today.

INTERVIEWER: _____ they _____ the computer?

3. (replace)

SCIENTIST: No, they _____ the computer, but one day robots _____
4. (replace)

probably _____ computers.
5. (operate)

INTERVIEWER: That's amazing! What other things _____ personal robots

_____?
6. (do)

SCIENTIST: Well, for one thing, they _____ complete home entertainment
7. (be)

centers. They _____, they _____ . . .
8. (sing)   9. (dance)

INTERVIEWER: _____ they _____ jokes?
10. (tell)

SCIENTIST: Yes, they _____! But, as with humans, they _____
11.

always _____ funny!
12. (be)

INTERVIEWER: What else _____ personal robots _____?
13. (do)

_____ they _____ more serious uses?
14. (have)

SCIENTIST: Yes, they _____. Robots _____ probably
15.

_____ care for this country's aging population. I don't believe they
16. (help)

_____ people, but they _____ some of the more
17. (replace)   18. (perform)

routine activities such as making the bed and loading the dishwasher.

INTERVIEWER: It all sounds great. Do you predict any problems?

SCIENTIST: Unfortunately, yes. Some people _____ happy with the spread of
19. (be)

robots. Not everyone's life _____. Some people _____
20. (improve)   21. (lose)

their jobs to robots. And other people _____ criminal robots!
22. (create)

INTERVIEWER: _____ we _____ new laws to deal with robotic crime?
23. (need)

SCIENTIST: I'm afraid so.

INTERVIEWER: Tell me, how _____ these personal robots _____?
24. (look)

SCIENTIST: Well, they _____ exactly like humans, but they _____
25. (look)   26. (resemble)

us quite a bit.

INTERVIEWER: And when _____ all this _____?
27. (happen)

SCIENTIST: Soon! I predict it _____ in the very near future.
28. (happen)

5 | RECOGNIZING THE SIMPLE PRESENT AND PRESENT PROGRESSIVE WHEN THEY REFER TO THE FUTURE

Read this article about a new play. Underline the simple present and present progressive verbs only when they refer to the future.

CURTAIN CALL

A NEW PLAY

ROBOTS

Next Wednesday <u>is</u> the first performance of *Robots*. Melissa Robins is playing the leading role. Robins, who lives in Italy and who is vacationing in Greece, is not available for an interview at this time. She is, however, appearing on Channel 8's "Theater Talk" sometime next month.

Although shows traditionally begin at 8:00 P.M., *Robots*, because of its length, starts half an hour earlier.

Immediately following the opening-night performance, the company is having a reception in the theater lounge. Tickets are still available. Call 555-6310 for more information.

6 | CONTRAST OF FUTURE FORMS

Some people are flying to San Francisco. Read the conversations and circle the most appropriate future forms.

1. **A:** Do you know our arrival time?

   B: According to the schedule, (we arrive) / we'll arrive at 10:45.

2. **A:** Why did you bring your computer with you?

   B: <u>I'll do / I'm going to do</u> some work while we're away.

3. **A:** I'm thirsty. I think <u>I'll ask / I'm asking</u> for a soda.

   B: Good idea. There's the flight attendant.

4. **A:** Excuse me. Do you know what the weather is like in San Francisco?

   B: It's clear now, but <u>it's raining / it's going to rain</u> tomorrow.

5. **A:** Oh, good! <u>They'll show / They're showing</u> the new *Star Wars* on today's flight.

   B: Great! I missed it when it was playing in the theaters.

6. **A:** Just look at those dark clouds!

   B: I see. It looks like <u>we're going to have / we'll have</u> some rough weather ahead.

7. **A:** Hold on to your cup! It looks like <u>it will spill / it's going to spill</u>.

   B: I've got it. This sure is a bumpy flight!

   A: I know. <u>I'll be / I'm</u> glad to be back on the ground again.

8. **A:** I'm tired. I think <u>I'll take / I'm taking</u> a little nap. Wake me when the movie begins.

   B: OK. Sweet dreams.

9. **A:** It's 11:00 P.M. already!

   B: I know. <u>We're going to arrive / We arrive</u> late.

   A: That's too bad.

10. **A:** You know, I don't think the airport buses run after midnight.

    B: I'm afraid you're right. How <u>are we going to get / are we getting</u> to the hotel?

11. **A:** Hmmm. No buses. Well, that's no problem. <u>We'll take / We're going to take</u> a taxi.

    B: Do you think there <u>will still be / are still</u> taxis in front of the terminal so late?

    A: Oh, sure.

    B: That's good.

12. **A:** I missed the announcement. What did the captain say?

    B: He said, "Fasten your seat belts. <u>We're landing / We'll land</u> in about 10 minutes."

    A: Great.

13. **C:** How long <u>are you going to stay / will you stay</u> in San Francisco?

    A: Just a week.

    C: Well, enjoy yourselves. And thank you for flying FairAir.

14. **A:** Maybe <u>we'll see / we're seeing</u> you on the return flight!

    C: Maybe!

7 | EDITING

Read this boy's postcard. There are five mistakes in the use of future forms. The first mistake is already corrected. Find and correct four more. Note: There may be more than one way to correct the mistakes!

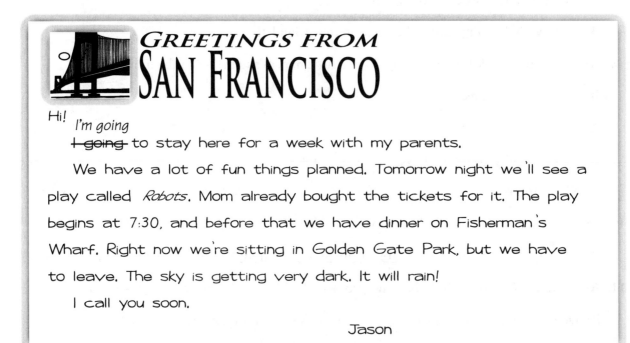

GREETINGS FROM
SAN FRANCISCO

Hi!
~~I going~~ *I'm going* to stay here for a week with my parents.

We have a lot of fun things planned. Tomorrow night we'll see a play called *Robots*. Mom already bought the tickets for it. The play begins at 7:30, and before that we have dinner on Fisherman's Wharf. Right now we're sitting in Golden Gate Park, but we have to leave. The sky is getting very dark. It will rain!

I call you soon.

Jason

8 | PERSONALIZATION

Write a note to a friend. Tell your friend about your future plans.

_____

_____

_____

_____

_____

_____

_____

_____

_____

Future Time Clauses

1 | SIMPLE PRESENT OR FUTURE WITH *WILL*

Complete the clauses with the correct form of the verbs in parentheses. Use the future or the simple present. Then match the time clauses to the main clauses.

Time Clause

_h_ 1. When the alarm clock _____*rings*_____ at 7:00 A.M.,
(ring)

_____ 2. After she _____,
(get up)

_____ 3. As soon as the coffee _____ ready,
(be)

_____ 4. While they _____ breakfast,
(eat)

_____ 5. When they _____ breakfast,
(finish)

_____ 6. After her husband _____ the dinner dishes,
(wash)

_____ 7. As soon as they _____ the car,
(get in)

_____ 8. Until he _____ his driver's license,
(get)

_____ 9. Until the rain _____,
(stop)

_____ 10. By the time the day _____ over,
(be)

Main Clause

a. they _____ very
(be)
tired.

b. she _____.
(drive)

c. they _____ it.
(drink)

d. they _____ their
(fasten)
seat belts.

e. she _____ them.
(dry)

f. they _____ their
(need)
umbrellas.

g. they _____ dishes.
(do)

h. she _____*'ll get up*_____.
(get up)

i. she _____ a shower.
(take)

j. they _____ the
(read)
morning newspaper.

2 | SIMPLE PRESENT OR FUTURE (*WILL* / *BE GOING TO*) AND TIME EXPRESSIONS

Vera is a student. Look at her future plans. Complete the sentences below with the correct form of the verbs in parentheses. Use Vera's plans to choose the correct time expression.

> ### Future Plans
> Take the TOEFL* exam
> Apply to college for next year
> Finish school
> Visit Aunt Isabel
> Get a summer job and take a computer-
>   programming course
> Fly to Brazil – Aug. 28
> Get married – Sept. 30
> Return to the United States
> Move into new apartment
> Look for a part-time job

*TOEFL® = Test of English as a Foreign Language

1. Vera _____will take_____ the TOEFL® exam _____before_____ she _____applies_____
              (take)   (when / before)   (apply)
   to college.

2. Vera _____ to college _____ she _____ school.
        (apply)   (before / after)   (finish)

3. _____ she _____ school, she _____ her aunt.
   (Before / After)   (finish)   (visit)

4. _____ she _____ at a summer job, she _____ a
   (Before / While)   (work)   (take)
   course in computer programming.

5. She _____ her aunt Isabel _____ she _____ a job.
     (visit)   (while / before)   (get)

6. _____ she _____ the course, she _____ to Brazil.
   (Before / When)   (finish)   (fly)

7. She _____ _____ she _____ in Brazil.
   (get married)   (when / before)   (be)

8. She _____ to the United States _____ she _____.
   (return)   (before / after)   (get married)

9. She _____ into a new apartment _____ she _____
   (move)   (when / while)   (return)
   to the United States.

10. _____ she _____ into a new apartment, she _____
    (Before / After)   (move)   (look for)
    a part-time job.

3 | SENTENCE COMBINING

Combine these pairs of sentences. Use the future or the simple present form of the verb. Remember to use commas when necessary.

1. Vera will finish her summer job. Then she's going to fly to Brazil.

   _____*Vera is going to fly to Brazil*_____ after _____*she finishes her summer job.*_____

2. Vera will save enough money from her job. Then she's going to buy a plane ticket.

   As soon as _____

3. Vera's going to buy presents for her family. Then she's going to go home.

   Before _____

4. Vera will arrive at the airport. Her father will be there to drive her home.

   When _____

5. Vera and her father will get home. They'll immediately have dinner.

   As soon as _____

6. They'll finish dinner. Then Vera will give her family the presents.

   _____ after _____

7. Vera's brother will wash the dishes, and Vera's sister will dry them.

   _____ while _____

8. The whole family will stay up talking. Then the clock will strike midnight.

   _____ until _____

9. They'll all feel very tired. Then they'll go to bed.

   By the time _____

10. Vera's head will hit the pillow, and she'll fall asleep immediately.

    _____ as soon as _____

11. Vera will wake up the next morning. She'll call her friends.

    When _____

12. She'll have breakfast. Then she'll see her friends.

    _____ as soon as _____

4 | EDITING

Read Vera's e-mail. There are eight mistakes in the use of future time clauses. The first one is already corrected. Find and correct seven more. Remember to look at punctuation!

Hi, Monica!

I'm really looking forward to your arrival tomorrow. Before you ~~will~~ know it, you'll be here!

After I will pick you up at the airport, we'll go straight to my parents' house. My mother is

going to make a special dinner, but before we have dinner, you and I go for a drive with

Paulo. Rio is a beautiful city, and we can't wait to show you some of the sights. After we will

have dinner some of our friends will come over to meet you.

Let's talk on the phone once more, before you're going to leave. I'm going out for a few

hours, but I call you as soon as I get back.

I'll speak to you soon.

Vera

5 | PERSONALIZATION

Complete these sentences with information about your own future plans.

1. As soon as _____, I'll go to bed.

2. Before I take a break, _____.

3. Until _____, I'll stay in school.

4. When I save enough money, _____.

5. I won't _____ before I _____.

6. _____ after _____.

7. _____ while _____.

8. When I finish this exercise, _____.

Wh- Questions: Subject and Object

1 | QUESTIONS ABOUT THE SUBJECT

Ask questions about the words in italics. Use **What**, **Whose**, **Who**, *or* **How many**.

1. *Something* happened last night.

   _What happened last night?_____

2. *Someone's* phone rang at midnight.

   _____

3. *Someone* was calling for Michelle.

   _____

4. *Someone* was having a party.

   _____

5. *Some number of* people left the party.

   _____

6. *Something* surprised them.

   _____

7. *Someone's* friend called the police.

   _____

8. *Some number of* police arrived.

   _____

9. *Something* happened next.

   _____

10. *Someone* told the police about a theft.

    _____

(continued)

11. *Someone's* jewelry disappeared.

_____

12. *Some number of* necklaces vanished.

_____

2 | QUESTIONS ABOUT THE OBJECT AND *WHY, WHEN,* OR *WHERE*

Use the cues to write questions about Megan Knight, an accountant in Texas. Then match the questions and answers.

Questions	Answers
_e_ **1.** Where / she / live?	**a.** Two years.
Where does she live?	**b.** By bus.
2. How many rooms / her apartment / have?	**c.** The first of the month.
_____	**d.** Ling, Jackson, & Drew, Inc.
3. How much rent / she / pay?	**e.** In Texas.
_____	**f.** Five and a half.
4. When / she / pay the rent?	**g.** She's an accountant.
_____	**h.** Her sister.
5. Who / she / live with?	**i.** Because she doesn't like to drive.
_____	**j.** About $800 a month.
6. What / she / do?	
_____	
7. Which company / she / work for?	
_____	
8. How long / she / plan to stay there?	
_____	
9. How / she / get to work?	
_____	
10. Why / she / take the bus?	
_____	

3 | QUESTIONS ABOUT THE SUBJECT AND OBJECT AND *WHY, WHEN,* OR *WHERE*

Megan wrote a letter to her friend Janice. The letter got wet, and now Janice can't read some parts of it. What questions does Janice ask to get the missing information?

Dear Janice,

Hi! I just moved to ⎯⎯⎯⎯⎯⎯. I left Chicago because ⎯⎯⎯⎯⎯⎯.
1.   **2.**

⎯⎯⎯⎯ moved with me, and we are sharing an apartment. I got a job in a ⎯⎯⎯⎯⎯.
3.   **4.**

It started ⎯⎯⎯⎯. The people seem nice. Our apartment is great. It has ⎯⎯⎯ rooms.
5.   **6.**

⎯⎯⎯⎯ of the rooms came with carpeting, but two of them have beautiful wood floors. The rent
7.

isn't too high, either. We each pay $⎯⎯ a month.
8.

We need to buy some ⎯⎯⎯⎯⎯. ⎯⎯⎯⎯⎯'s brother wants to visit her, so we really
9.   **10.**

need an extra bed.

By the way, ⎯⎯⎯⎯⎯ called last Sunday. I also spoke to ⎯⎯⎯⎯⎯. They
11.   **12.**

want to visit us in ⎯⎯⎯⎯. Would you like to come too? Is that a good time for you?
13.

There's plenty of room because ⎯⎯⎯⎯⎯⎯. Write and let me know.
14.

Love,
Megan

---

1. *Where did you move?* _____

2. _____

3. _____

4. _____

5. _____

6. _____

7. _____

8. _____

9. _____

10. _____

(continued)

11. _____

12. _____

13. _____

14. _____

4 | PERSONALIZATION

Imagine you are writing to a friend who has just moved. Ask your friend questions about his or her new home.

1. When _____

2. Where _____

3. Why _____

4. How many _____

5. What _____

6. How far _____

7. Which _____

8. Who _____

Reflexive and Reciprocal Pronouns

1 | REFLEXIVE PRONOUNS

Write the reflexive pronouns.

1. I _____ *myself* _____

2. my grandfather _____

3. the children _____

4. the class _____

5. my aunt _____

6. you _____ OR _____

7. people _____

8. life _____

9. my parents _____

10. we _____

2 | REFLEXIVE AND RECIPROCAL PRONOUNS

Choose the correct pronouns to complete the sentences.

1. Cindi and Jim phone each other / themselves every weekend.

2. They have worked with <u>each other / themselves</u> for five years.

3. Cindi <u>herself / himself</u> has been with the same company for 10 years.

4. It's a nice place. All of the employees consider <u>one another / themselves</u> lucky to be there.

5. They respect <u>each other / each other's</u> opinions.

6. The boss <u>herself / itself</u> is very nice.

7. She tells her employees, "Don't push <u>themselves / yourselves</u> too hard!"

(continued)

8. Cindi enjoys the job <u>herself / itself</u>, but she especially likes her co-workers.

9. My brother and I are considering applying for a job there <u>myself / ourselves</u>.

10. We talk to <u>each other / ourselves</u> about it when we jog together.

3 | REFLEXIVE AND RECIPROCAL PRONOUNS

Gina had a party. Read each conversation and complete the summary. Use the correct form of the verbs in parentheses with an appropriate reflexive or reciprocal pronoun.

1.   JOYCE: This party is a lot of fun.

     HANK: I've never danced with so any people in my life!

     SUMMARY: Joyce and Hank _____ *are enjoying themselves* _____ .
                                            (enjoy)

2.   RON: We were late because you forgot the address.

     MIA: It's not my fault. You never gave me the slip of paper!

     SUMMARY: Ron and Mia _____ .
                                        (criticize)

3.   GINA: I'm so glad you could come. There are food and drinks on that table over there.

            Why don't you take a plate and get some?

     CHEN: Thanks. I will. It all looks delicious.

     SUMMARY: Chen _____ .
                              (help)

4.   AMY: OK, Amy. Now don't be shy. Go over and talk to that guy over there.

     TIM: Come on, Tim. You can do it. She's looking in your direction. Just go on over.

     SUMMARY: Amy and Tim _____ .
                                    (talk)

5.   AMY: Hi. I'm Amy.

     TIM: Hi. I'm Tim.

     SUMMARY: Amy and Tim _____ .
                                    (introduce)

6.   AMY: So, how do you know Gina?

     TIM: Oh, Gina and I were in the same class. What about you?

     SUMMARY: Amy and Tim _____ .
                                    (talk)

7.   PAT: Did you come with Doug?

     LAURA: No. Doug couldn't make it, but he let me use his car.

     SUMMARY: Laura _____ .
                              (drive)

8.   **LIZ:** I'm sorry to hear about your job, Hank.

      HANK: I think I didn't take it seriously enough, but I've learned my lesson. I'll do better

      next time.

    SUMMARY: Hank _____ .
                                              (blame)

9.   **CARA:** You know, I'm really glad we met.

      LIZ: Me too. I feel like we've known each other a long time.

    SUMMARY: Cara and Liz _____ company.
                                              (enjoy)

10.   **LIZ:** It was a wonderful party. Thanks for inviting me.

      GINA: Thanks for coming. And thank you for the lovely flowers.

    SUMMARY: Liz and Gina _____ .
                                              (thank)

4 | EDITING

Read Liz's journal entry. There are eleven mistakes in the use of reflexive and reciprocal pronouns. The first mistake is already corrected. Find and correct ten more.

                                           April 25

                      myself

I really enjoyed ~~me~~ at Gina's party! Hank was there, and we talked to ourselves quite a bit. He's a little depressed about losing his job. The job himself wasn't that great, but he needs the money. He's disappointed in himself. He thinks it's all his own fault, and he blames him for the whole thing. Hank introduced myself to several of his friends. I spoke a lot to this one woman, Cara. We have a lot of things in common, and after just an hour, we felt like we had known each other's forever. Cara, himself, is a computer programmer, just like me.

    At first I was nervous about going to the party alone. I sometimes feel a little uncomfortable when I'm in a social situation by oneself. But this time was different. Before I went, I kept telling myself to relax. My roommate, too, kept telling myself, "Don't be so hard on you! Just have fun!" That's what I advised Hank to do too. Before we left the party, Hank and I promised us to keep in touch. I hope to see him again soon.

10 Phrasal Verbs

1 | PARTICLES

Complete the phrasal verbs with particles from the box. You will use some particles more than once.

back	down	in	off	on	out	over	together	up

Phrasal Verb   **Definition**

1. take _____*off*_____   *remove*

2. figure _____   *solve*

3. go _____   *continue*

4. call _____   *cancel*

5. call _____   *return a phone call*

6. fill _____   *complete*

7. turn _____   *reject*

8. point _____   *indicate*

9. grow _____   *become an adult*

10. give _____   *quit*

11. help _____   *assist*

12. blow _____   *explode*

13. look _____   *be careful*

14. come _____   *enter*

15. work _____   *exercise*

16. get _____   *return*

17. put _____   *assemble*

18. think _____   *consider*

2 | PHRASAL VERBS

Complete the handout for Professor Cho's class. Use the correct phrasal verbs from the box.

do over	hand in	help out	look over	look up
pick out	pic̶k̶ up	set up	talk over	write up

Science 101   Instructions for Writing the Term Paper   Prof. Cho

1. _____*Pick up*_____ a list of topics from the science department secretary.

2. _____ a topic that interests you. (If you are having problems choosing a topic,

    I'll be glad to _____ you _____ .)

3. Go online. Use the Internet to _____ information on your chosen topic.

4. _____ an appointment with me to _____ your topic.

5. _____ your first draft.

6. _____ it _____ carefully. Check for accuracy of facts, spelling,

    and grammar errors.

7. _____ your report _____ if necessary.

8. _____ it _____ by May 28.

---

3 | PHRASAL VERBS AND OBJECT PRONOUNS

Complete the conversations between roommates. Use phrasal verbs and pronouns.

1. **A:** I haven't picked up the list of topics for our science paper yet.

   B: I'll _____*pick it up*_____ for you. I'm going to the science

   office this afternoon.

2. **A:** Hey, guys. We've really got to clean up the kitchen. It's a mess.

   B: It's my turn to _____. I'll do it after dinner.

3. **A:** Did you remember to call your mom back?

   B: Oops! I'll _____ tonight.

(continued)

4. **A:** Hey, can you turn down that music? I'm trying to concentrate.

   B: Sorry. I'll _____ right away.

5. **A:** It's after 9:00. Do you think we should wake John up?

   B: Don't _____. He said he wanted to sleep late.

6. **A:** Professor Cho turned down my science topic.

   B: Really? Why did she _____?

7. **A:** When do we have to hand in our reports?

   B: We have to _____ by Friday.

8. **A:** I wanted to drop off my report this afternoon, but I'm not going to have time.

   B: I can _____ for you. I have an appointment

   with Professor Cho at noon.

4 | WORD ORDER

Professor Cho made a list of things to do with her class. Unscramble the words to make sentences. In some cases, more than one answer is possible.

1. the homework problems / back / give

   Give back the homework problems. OR *Give the homework problems back.*

2. out / common mistakes / point

   _____

3. them / over / talk

   _____

4. a new problem / out / pick

   _____

5. it / out / work / with the class

   _____

6. up / the results / write

   _____

7. go / to the next unit / on

   _____

8. up / the final exam questions / make

_____

9. them / out / hand

_____

10. study groups / up / set

_____

11. out / them / help

_____

12. Friday's class / off / call

_____

5 | EDITING

Read this student's e-mail. There are eleven mistakes in the use of phrasal verbs. The first mistake is already corrected. Find and correct ten more. A particle in the wrong place counts as one mistake.

Hi, Katy!

How are things going? I'm already into the second month of the spring semester, and I've

got a lot of work to do. For science class, I have to write a term paper. The professor made

 up
~~over~~ a list of possible topics. After looking over them, I think I've picked one out. I'm going to

write about chimpanzees. I've already looked some information about them online up. I

found up some very interesting facts.

Did you know that their hands look very much like their feet, and that they have fingernails

and toenails? Their thumbs and big toes are "opposable." This makes it easy for them to pick

things out with both their fingers and toes. Their arms are longer than their legs. This helps

---

(continued)

out them, too, because they can reach out to fruit growing on thin branches that would not otherwise support their weight. Adult males weigh between 90 and 115 pounds, and they are about four feet high when they stand out.

Like humans, chimpanzees are very social. They travel in groups called "communities." Mothers bring out their chimps, who stay with them until about the age of seven. Even after the chimps grow up, there is still a lot of contact with other chimpanzees.

I could go on, but I need to stop writing now so I can clean out my room (it's a mess!) a little before going to bed. It's late already, and I have to get early up tomorrow morning for my 9:00 class.

Please let me know how you are. Or call me. I'm often out, but if you leave a message, I'll call back you as soon as I can. It would be great to speak to you.

Best,

Tony

Ability:
Can, Could, Be able to

1 | AFFIRMATIVE AND NEGATIVE STATEMENTS WITH *CAN* AND *COULD*

Read about this student's ability in English. Then complete the statements for each item.
(For items 8–10, write complete statements.) Use **can**, **can't**, **could**, *or* **couldn't**.

Student's Name *Fernando Ochoa*

English Language Ability Questionnaire

Skill	Now	Before This Course
1. understand conversational English	✔	✘
2. understand recorded announcements	✘	✘
3. read an English newspaper	✔	✔
4. read an English novel	✘	✘
5. speak on the phone	✔	✘
6. speak with a group of people	✔	✘
7. write an e-mail	✔	✔
8. write a business letter	✘	✘
9. order a meal in English	✔	✔
10. go shopping	✔	✔

---

1. Before this course, he *couldn't understand conversational English.*

Now he *can understand conversational English.*

2. He *couldn't understand recorded anouncements* before the course, and

he still *can't understand recorded anouncements.*

3. He _____ now, and he

_____ before too.

4. He _____ before the course, and

he still _____.

(continued)

5. Now he _____, but before the course

   he _____.

6. Before the course, he _____, but

   now he _____.

7. Before the course, he _____.

   He still _____, of course.

8. _____

   _____

9. _____

   _____

10. _____

   _____

   SUMMARY: Fernando _____ do a lot more now than he

   _____ before the course.

2 | QUESTIONS AND ANSWERS WITH *CAN* AND *COULD*

A reporter from the school newspaper is interviewing a new student. Use **can** *or* **could** *and the words in parentheses to write the interview questions and the student's answers.*

1. (speak / any other languages)

   REPORTER: *Can you speak any other languages?* _____

   STUDENT: _____ *Yes, I can.* _____ I speak two other languages.

2. (What languages / speak)

   REPORTER: _____

   STUDENT: Spanish and French.

3. (speak Spanish / when you were a child)

   REPORTER: _____

   STUDENT: _____ I learned it as an adult.

4. (speak French)

REPORTER: _____

STUDENT: _____ We spoke French some of the time at home.

5. (before you came here / understand spoken English)

REPORTER: _____

STUDENT: _____ I didn't understand anything!

6. (understand song lyrics)

REPORTER: What about now? _____

STUDENT: _____ Especially if I listen to them more than once.

7. (before this course / write a business letter in English)

REPORTER: _____

STUDENT: _____ But I used to write in English to my friends.

8. (drive a car before you came here)

REPORTER: So, tell me some more about yourself. _____

_____

STUDENT: _____ I was too young.

9. (drive a car now)

REPORTER: _____

STUDENT: _____ I still haven't learned.

10. (swim)

REPORTER: We're not far from the beach here. _____

STUDENT: _____ I've been swimming since I was a little kid.

11. (surf before you came here)

REPORTER: What about surfing? _____

STUDENT: _____ But I learned to surf the first month I was here.

12. (What / do now / that / you / not do before)

REPORTER: _____

STUDENT: Oh! I _____ a lot of things now that I _____

before.

3 | AFFIRMATIVE AND NEGATIVE STATEMENTS WITH *BE ABLE TO*

*Read this article about hearing loss. Complete the article with the correct form of **be able to** and the verbs in parentheses.*

Living in a Hearing World

There are millions of people who have some degree of hearing loss. There are two major

types of hearing loss.

1. **Sound Sensitivity Loss.** People with this kind of loss _____*are not able to hear*_____
   1. (not hear)

   soft sounds—a whisper or a bird singing, for example. However, when sounds are loud

   enough, they _____ them correctly.
   2. (interpret)

2. **Sound Discrimination Loss.** People with this particular kind of hearing loss

   _____ one sound from another. As a result of this,
   3. (not distinguish)

   they _____ speech—even when it is loud enough for
   4. (not understand)

   them to hear.

   How do people with hearing disabilities get along in a hearing world? Most people with

hearing impairments _____ some sounds. With the use of
5. (hear)

hearing aids and cochlear implants (devices put in the ear during an operation), many people

_____ some of their ability to hear. Some people with
6. (get back)

hearing disabilities _____ lips. But, at best, lipreading is
7. (read)

only 30 to 50 percent effective. Even a good lip-reader _____
8. (not recognize)

all the sounds. Just ask someone to silently mouth the words *pat*, *bat*, and *mat*. The

three words sound different, but they all *look* the same. In addition, the human eye

_____ fast enough to process speech by vision alone. By
9. (not work)

far the most successful form of communication is signing—the use of sign language. People

with hearing impairments _____ successfully with others
10. (communicate)

who know this language.

4 | QUESTIONS AND SHORT ANSWERS WITH *BE ABLE TO*

Modern technology can make life easier for people with hearing loss. Read this FAQ (frequently asked questions) about assisted-hearing devices. Use **will be able to** *to complete the questions and write short answers.*

Q: My daughter has a hearing disability. She's going to have her first child next month.

    <u>*Will*</u> she <u>   *be able to know*   </u> when the baby is crying?
                                        1. (know)

A: <u>   *Yes, she will.*   </u> She can get a device that flashes lights (so she'll be
                 2.

able to see the signal) or vibrates (so she'll be able to feel the signal).

******

Q: My nephew can't hear the alarm clock in the morning. I want to buy him a flashing lamp.

    <u>   </u> he <u>   </u> it when he's sleeping?
                        3. (How / see)

A: You can see a strong light through your eyelids—as long as you don't have your head under

the covers!

******

Q: I'm thinking of getting a cochlear implant. <u>   </u> I <u>   </u>
                                                       4. (hear)

"normally" with it?

A: <u>   </u> Hearing with an implant is not the same as
                 5.

"normal" hearing, but it *can* help a lot.

******

Q: I just moved into a new apartment, and I'm having trouble hearing the doorbell.

    <u>   </u> I <u>   </u> this problem without disturbing my
                        6. (How / solve)

neighbors?

A: You can get a system that produces sound in different locations in your apartment—not just

at the front door.

******

(continued)

Q: My husband and I both wear hearing aids, and we both love to travel. _____ we

_____ the theater when we're in London next summer?
7. (enjoy)

A: _____ Theaters in London use a "loop" system. This
8.

system sends sounds directly to your hearing aid (without wires!). You just need to set your

hearing aid to "T." Have a good trip!

5 | CONTRAST: *CAN* AND *BE ABLE TO*

*Read this article about a well-known actress who is deaf. Complete the story with the
correct form of **can**, **could**, or **be able to** and the verbs in parentheses. Use **can** or **could**
when possible.*

Actress Marlee Matlin _____*could hear*_____ at birth but lost
1. (hear)

her hearing at the age of 18 months as a result of a childhood illness.

By the age of five, she _____ lips. Shortly
2. (read)

after that, she mastered sign language. At first, Matlin felt angry and

frightened by her hearing impairment. "I wanted to be perfect, and I

_____ my deafness," she said during an
3. (not accept)

interview. With time, however, she learned to accept it.

Matlin began her acting career at the age of eight, when she performed in theater for the deaf.

In 1986, she received an Oscar nomination for best actress in the Hollywood film *Children of a

Lesser God*. In the movie she played the role of an angry woman who was deaf and did not want

to speak. For Matlin, however, speaking is very important. At the Oscar ceremonies, she

_____ her award verbally. It was the first time the public heard her speak.
4. (accept)

"It's what I wanted to do, because a lot of people all over the world _____
5. (see)

me for who I am," she said. Matlin was worried, however. She asked, "What other roles

_____ I _____ in the future?"
6. (do)

Matlin didn't need to worry. She continued to receive important roles in movies and on TV.

One reviewer said "She _____ more saying nothing than most people
7. (do)

_____ talking." Today, thanks to intensive speech training, she
         8. (do)

_____ very clearly. In 1994 she _____ something
         9. (speak)   **10. (achieve)**

for the first time: She played the role of a character who was not deaf. Matlin, in fact, doesn't

think of herself as a "deaf actress." She's an "actress who happens to be deaf." She hopes that in

the future she _____ more roles that are not specifically for people with
                        11. (get)

hearing impairments.

In addition to her acting career, Matlin is actively trying to improve lives. In 1995, she helped

get an important law passed in the United States. As a result of this law, today most TV sets have

closed-captioning on their screens so that hearing-impaired viewers _____
                                                                            12. (read)

everything. Matlin does not believe in limits. "I _____ attitudes on
                                                        13. (change)

deafness and prove we _____ everything—except hear," she said.
                              14. (do)

6 | EDITING

Read this student's composition. There are ten mistakes in the use of **can**, **could**, *and*
be able to. *The first one is already corrected. Find and correct nine more.*

>   *couldn't*
> Before I came to this country, I ~~can't~~ do many things in English. For example,
> I couldn't follow a conversation if many people were talking at the same time. I
> remember a party I went to. Everyone was speaking English, and I wasn't able
> understand a word! I felt so uncomfortable. Finally, my aunt came to pick me up,
> and I could leave the party.
>   Today I can to understand much better. I am taking classes at the adult center.
> My teacher is very good. She can explains things well, and she always gives us
> the chance to talk a lot in class. When I finish this class, I can speak and
> understand a lot better.
>   Be able to speak English well is very important to me. I practice a lot at home
> too. When I first came to this country, I can't understand very much TV, but now I
> can to understand much better. In fact, I can do a lot now, and I think in a few more
> months I can do even more.

7 | PERSONALIZATION

Look at the English Language Ability Questionnaire in Exercise 1. Write sentences about your English ability now and before this course.

1. _____

   _____

2. _____

   _____

3. _____

   _____

4. _____

   _____

Permission: *Can, Could, May, Do you mind if*

1 | QUESTIONS AND RESPONSES

Match these classroom questions and responses.

Questions

__d__ **1.** Do you mind if I bring my friends
   to class?

_____ **2.** May I ask a question?

_____ **3.** Do you mind if I record the lesson?

_____ **4.** Could I open the window?

_____ **5.** Can we review Unit 4?

_____ **6.** May I leave the room?

_____ **7.** Could we use our dictionaries?

_____ **8.** Could I borrow a pen?

Responses

a. Certainly. The key to the restroom is hanging
   on the wall.

b. Not at all. I think it's a good idea.

c. Sure. I hope I can answer it.

d. Sorry, but yes, I do. It's already pretty
   crowded.

e. Sure. But remember: You don't have to look
   up every word.

f. I'm afraid we can't. We're running out of time.

g. Sure. But please remember to return it.

h. Go right ahead. It's quite warm in here.

2 | QUESTIONS

Read the classroom situations. Complete the questions asking for permission.

1. You want to open the window.

   May *I open the window?* _____

2. Your whole class wants to review Unit 6.

   Could _____

3. You want to borrow a classmate's pen.

   Can _____

(continued)

4. You want to look at someone's class notes.

   Do you mind if _____

5. You want to come late to the next class.

   Do you mind if _____

6. Your roommate wants to come to the next class with you.

   Could _____

7. You want to ask a question.

   May _____

8. You and a classmate would like to use a dictionary.

   Can _____

9. You and your classmates want to leave five minutes early.

   Could _____

10. Your sister wants to go on the class trip with the rest of the class.

    Do you mind if _____

3 | PERSONALIZATION

Imagine that you are in class and are in the following situations. Ask your teacher for permission to do something.

1. You don't understand something the teacher is saying.

   _____

2. You don't feel well.

   _____

3. Your cousin (from your country) is going to visit you for a week.

   _____

4. You're having trouble with a paper you're writing.

   _____

Now write your own request.

5. _____

4 | AFFIRMATIVE AND NEGATIVE STATEMENTS

Look at the flyer. Complete the statements with the words in parentheses.

Class Trip

You are invited to our annual class picnic on

Sunday, May 26, at Glenwood State Park.

Food and beverages welcome, but no glass containers, please!

Bus tickets $5.00 (check or cash)

Advance purchase only • No refunds

Bring a friend!

Don't forget your bathing suit! The lake is beautiful.

1. You _____*may bring*_____ a friend.
   (may / bring)

2. You _____ your own food.
   (can / bring)

3. You _____ your own drinks.
   (can / bring)

4. You _____ juice from a glass bottle at the picnic.
   (can / drink)

5. You _____ for your bus ticket by check.
   (can / pay)

6. You _____ for your bus ticket by cash.
   (can / pay)

7. You _____ for your ticket by credit card.
   (may / pay)

8. You _____ your bus ticket on the day of the trip.
   (may / purchase)

9. You _____ a refund.
   (can / get)

10. You _____ in the lake.
   (may / swim)

5 | EDITING

*Read this professor's response to an e-mail from one of his students. (The professor's answers are in **bold** print.) There are six mistakes in making and responding to requests. The first one is already corrected. Find and correct five more.*

Subj: Missed classes—Reply
Date: 04-23-06 11:22:43 EST
From: profwilson@bryant.edu
To: Timbotwo@hotline.com

>>>Timbotwo@hotline.com> 04/23/06 9:05am>>>

Professor Wilson—

I've been sick for the past two days. That's why I missed the last test.
            take
May I ~~taking~~ a make-up exam?

Yes. If you bring a doctor's note.

If I can take the exam, may I use my calculator during the test?

No, you mayn't! I did not allow calculators during this test.

Could my roommate comes to class and take notes for me on Thursday?

Yes, he could.

Do you mind when he records the class for me?

Not at all. It's fine for him to record the class.

One last thing—I know I missed some handouts. May I have please copies of them?

Sure. I'll give them to your roommate on Thursday.

Thanks a lot.

Tim

Requests: *Can, Could, Will, Would, Would you mind*

1 | REQUESTS AND RESPONSES

Match these office requests and responses.

Requests	Responses
_d_ 1. Could you meet me tomorrow at 8:00 A.M.?	a. I'd be glad to. When do you need it?
____ 2. Will you please type this memo for me?	b. Sure. It is pretty cold in here.
____ 3. Could you show me how to use the scanner?	c. Of course I can. When would you like to reschedule it?
____ 4. Would you please spell your last name for me?	d. I'm sorry. I have an early-morning dentist appointment.
____ 5. Would you mind mailing this letter for me?	e. Sure. It's Djohn@iol.com.
____ 6. Can you cancel tomorrow's meeting for me? I have to go out of town.	f. Sure. . . . Hello, J and R Equities.
____ 7. Will you shut the window, please?	g. Sure. It's M-A-R-D-J-A-I-T.
____ 8. Would you get that box down from the closet?	h. Sorry, but I don't know how. Ask Todd.
____ 9. Could you get the phone for me?	i. I'd like to, but it's too heavy for me to lift.
____ 10. Can you give me Doug Johnson's e-mail address?	j. Not at all.

Write the numbers of the responses that mean "Yes": _2,_ _____

Write the numbers of the responses that mean "No": _____

Write the number of the response that has a negative word, but means

"OK, I'll do it.": _____

2 | REQUESTS

These conversations take place in an office. Use the correct form of the phrases in the box to complete the requests.

~~answer the phone~~	keep the noise down
buy some stamps	lend me $5.00
come to my office	open the window
explain this note to me	pick up a sandwich
get Frank's phone number	stay late tonight

1. **A:** Could you _____*answer the phone*_____? My hands are full.

   B: Sure. I'll get it.

2. **A:** Would you mind _____? It's really hot in here.

   B: No, not at all.

3. **A:** Can you please _____ for me?

   B: Certainly. I pass the post office on my way home.

4. **A:** I'm going to the coffee shop. Can I get you anything?

   B: Could you _____ for me?

5. **A:** Would you mind _____? We really have to get this

   report done by tomorrow.

   B: I'm sorry, but I have to visit my aunt in the hospital.

6. **A:** Will you _____, please? I can't hear myself think!

   B: Sorry!

7. **A:** Can you _____ when you have the chance?

   B: Sure. I'll be right there.

8. **A:** Would you _____ for me?

   B: It's 555-4345.

9. **A:** Would you mind _____?

   B: Not at all. What don't you understand?

10. **A:** Could you _____?

    B: Oh, I'm sorry. I'm short on cash.

3 | WORD ORDER

Unscramble the words to make requests. Use the correct form of the verbs.

1. come / can / please / here / you

   Can you please come here?

2. work / on Saturday / would you mind

   _____

3. you / me / please / will / help

   _____

4. would / please / explain / you / this

   _____

5. drive / home / you / me / please / could

   _____

4 | EDITING

Read the office notes below and on page 66. There are six mistakes in making requests. The first mistake is already corrected. Find and correct five more. Don't forget to check punctuation.

1.

Meng,
                    file
Would you ~~filed~~ these,
please?

Thanks.

R.L.

2.

write it down

Hi Ted,
   Could you please remember to turn off the lights when you leave?
                    Thanks,
                    Lynn

(continued)

3.

HANK,

WILL YOU RETURN PLEASE THE STAPLER?

BRAD

4.

Melida,

Can you make 5 copies of these pages, please?

Thanks,

Ellen

5.

John,

Would you mind leave the finished report on my desk?

Rey

6.

Celia,
Could you please remember to lock the door.
Thank you.

Diana

7.

Annie,
Would you please to call Ms. Rivera before the end of the day?

Thanks,
JJ

8.

Todd —
Could you print out 10 copies of the Hendricks report?
Also, would you mind to e-mail Lisa Barker a copy?

Thanks a lot.
Heather

5 | PERSONALIZATION

Write one request that you would like to make of each of the following people.

1. (To your teacher) _____

_____

2. (To a classmate) _____

_____

3. (To a friend) _____

_____

4. (To your boss) _____

_____

5. (To your landlord) _____

_____

6. (To _____) _____

_____

14 Advice: *Should, Ought to, Had better*

1 | AFFIRMATIVE AND NEGATIVE STATEMENTS WITH *SHOULD*

Rewrite these cell-phone tips. Give advice with **should**. *Choose between affirmative and negative.*

CELL-PHONE ETIQUETTE

Cell phones are wonderful, but they can also be very annoying.
Here are some rules you should follow to be polite.

📱 Turn off your cell phone in public places such as movie theaters and class.

1. *You should turn off your cell phone in public places such as movie theaters and class.*

📱 Don't shout into the phone.

2. _____

📱 Speak in a quiet, normal voice.

3. _____

📱 Leave the room to make a phone call.

4. _____

📱 Don't discuss private issues in public places.

5. _____

📱 Don't stand too close to other people when you are talking on the phone.

6. _____

📱 Pay attention to other people on the street when you are walking and talking.

7. _____

📱 Never dial while you are driving.

8. _____

2 | AFFIRMATIVE AND NEGATIVE STATEMENTS WITH *SHOULD, OUGHT TO, HAD BETTER*

Complete these conversations with the correct form of the verbs in parentheses. Choose between affirmative and negative. Use contractions when possible.

1. **A:** Excuse me, but you really _____*shouldn't use*_____ your cell phone in here.
   (should / use)

   The sign says "No cell phones."

   B: Sorry. I didn't see the sign.

2. **A:** You _____ Aunt Rosa. I know she'd be happy to hear from you.
   (should / call)

   B: Good idea. I'll call her as soon as I get off the phone with you.

3. **A:** You _____ to pick up some milk on the way home. We're all out
   (had better / forget)

   of it, and we need it for dinner.

   B: Call me again to remind me. OK?

4. **A:** We _____ the movie at Cinema Village Saturday night. I hear it's
   a. (ought to / see)

   really great.

   B: OK. But we _____ tickets sometime in the afternoon, or it'll be
   b. (had better / buy)

   hard to get in.

5. **A:** We _____ that restaurant near the theater.
   (should / try)

   B: Good idea. I'll call and make a reservation.

6. **A:** Our cell-phone bill is really high. I think we _____ about changing
   a. (ought to / think)

   calling plans.

   B: You're right. We _____ it.
   b. (should / look into)

7. **A:** People really _____ on their cell phones while they're driving. It's
   a. (should / talk)

   really dangerous.

   B: You know, it's illegal in many places.

   A: Well, there _____ a law against it here too.
   b. (should / be)

8. **A:** You _____ Andy now. He's probably already asleep.
   (had better / call)

   B: OK. I'll call him tomorrow.

(continued)

9. **A:** They _____ a "quiet car" on this train. It's hard to work with all
   (ought to / have)
   these people talking on their cells.

   B: That's a great idea.

10. **A:** I _____ call-waiting on my cell phone. I'm missing too many calls.
    (should / get)
    B: I'm surprised you don't have it already.

11. **A:** I _____ so loud. I think I'm disturbing people around me.
    (should / talk)
    B: Just call me when you get home. OK?

12. **A:** It's 7:00. I _____ now. I don't want to be late.
    (had better / hang up)
    B: OK. Talk to you later.

3 | QUESTIONS AND ANSWERS WITH *SHOULD*

Read this invitation. Use the words in parentheses and the information in the invitation to complete the phone conversation.

YOU ARE INVITED TO A PARTY!

FOR: Scott's SURPRISE birthday barbecue

DATE: June 11

TIME: 2:00 P.M. sharp!

PLACE: 20 Greenport Avenue

RSVP by May 15. Please don't call here!
Call Amy's cell phone and leave a message.
500-555-3234.
No gifts, please!
(but please bring something to drink)

LISA: Hi, Tania.

TANIA: Hi, Lisa. What's up?

LISA: Aunt Rosa's having a birthday party for Uncle Scott. She didn't have your new address, so she asked me to call and invite you. It's on June 11. Can you come?

TANIA: Sure. Just give me all the information. (What time / be there)

What time should I be there?
_____
1.

LISA: Let's see. I have the invitation right here.

_____*You should be there at 2:00 P.M. sharp.*_____
                                                    2.

TANIA: (What / wear)

_____
                                                    3.

LISA: Something casual. It's a barbecue.

TANIA: (bring a gift)

_____
                                                    4.

LISA: _____ The invitation says "No gifts."
                          5.

TANIA: OK. What about food? (bring something to eat or drink)

_____
                                                    6.

LISA: _____
                                                    7.

Oh, and the invitation says "RSVP." In other words, Aunt Rosa wants a response.

TANIA: (When / respond)

_____
                                                    8.

LISA: _____
                                                    9.

TANIA: (call Aunt Rosa)

_____
                                                    10.

LISA: _____ I forgot to tell you. It's a surprise party!
                          11.

TANIA: OK. (Who / call)

_____
                                                    12.

LISA: _____
                                                    13.

TANIA: Fine. Sounds like fun. I'll see you there. Thanks for calling.

LISA: No problem. See you there.

4 | EDITING

*Read this quiz. There are ten mistakes in the use of **should**, **ought to**, and **had better**.*
The first mistake is already corrected. Find and correct nine more.

Party Etiquette Quiz

Do you know what you should do at a party? Check the best answer.

1. You are at a party and you can't remember someone's name. What ~~you should~~ *should you* do?

☐ **a.** You should no ask the person's name.

☐ **b.** You better leave immediately!

☐ **c.** You ought just ask.

2. You don't know anyone at the party, and your host doesn't introduce you to the other guests. Had you better introduce yourself?

☐ **a.** Yes, you should. You should say, "Hi. My name's _____."

☐ **b.** No, you should. You'd better tell the host to introduce you.

3. Your cell phone rings during the party. You should answer it?

☐ **a.** Just let it ring. You had not better answer it.

☐ **b.** You should answer it, but just have a short conversation.

☐ **c.** You really ought to leave the room and speak to the person in private.

4. You had a very nice time at the party. How you should thank your host?

☐ **a.** You should just say "thank you" when you leave.

☐ **b.** You should send a "thank you" e-mail the next day.

☐ **c.** You oughta write a long "thank you" letter and send a gift too.

5 | PERSONALIZATION

A friend of yours is going to a party. He or she won't know anyone there and feels a little
nervous. Write five sentences giving your friend advice. Use your own paper.

Suggestions: *Let's, Could, Why don't, Why not, How about*

1 | SUGGESTIONS

Match the two halves of each suggestion. Notice the end punctuation—period (.) or question mark (?).

__c__ 1. My feet hurt. Why don't we

_____ 2. The weather's terrible. How about

_____ 3. We have an hour before the show starts. We could

_____ 4. You look exhausted. Why don't I

_____ 5. This concert is terrible. Let's not

_____ 6. I'm really hungry. How about

_____ 7. There's so much to see! How about

_____ 8. If John's unhappy at the Blue Water Inn, why doesn't he

_____ 9. It's going to be hot tomorrow. Let's

_____ 10. There's a gift shop. Maybe we could

a. going to a movie?

b. have a cup of coffee.

c. take a taxi?

d. go to the beach.

e. getting a slice of pizza?

f. change hotels?

g. meet you back at the hotel?

h. buy some souvenirs there.

i. taking a walking tour?

j. stay until the end.

2 | PUNCTUATION

Circle the correct phrase to complete these conversations between tourists on vacation. Add the correct punctuation: period (.) or question mark (?).

1. **A:** I'm exhausted. We've been walking for hours.

   B: How about / (Why don't we) sit on that bench for a while _?_

2. **A:** I'm almost out of film.

   B: There's a drugstore over there. Maybe you could / Let's not get film there __

(continued)

3. **A:** It would be nice to see some of the countryside.

   B: <u>Let's / How about</u> rent a car __

4. **A:** <u>Why not / How about</u> taking a bus tour __

   B: That's a good idea. It's less expensive than renting a car.

5. **A:** I want to take a picture of that building. <u>Why don't you / How about</u> stand in front of it __

   B: OK.

6. **A:** We have an hour before we have to meet the rest of our tour group.

   B: <u>Let's / Let's not</u> get a cup of coffee in that café __

   A: Good idea. I could use something to drink.

7. **A:** I heard it's going to rain tomorrow.

   B: <u>Maybe we could / How about</u> go to a museum __

8. **A:** You know, Sara really enjoys going to museums.

   B: <u>Why don't / Why doesn't</u> she come with us __

9. **A:** I really need to get a better map of the city.

   B: <u>Why don't you / Let's not</u> stop at that tourist information office __

   I'm sure they have maps.

10. **A:** I don't know what to get for my daughter.

    B: <u>Why don't you / How about</u> getting one of those sweatshirts __

11. **A:** I'm tired, and my feet are starting to hurt.

    B: <u>Maybe we could / How about</u> sit on one of those benches over there __

12. **A:** Look at that beautiful building. Why don't you take a picture of it?

    B: <u>That's a good idea / Because I don't want to</u> __

3 | SUGGESTIONS

Look at the tourist flyer. Use the suggestions in the flyer to complete the conversation.

BOSTON Highlights

Here are some of the many things you can do in this "capital of New England":

☐ **Go to Haymarket**—open-air fruit and vegetable stands (Fridays and Saturdays only).

☑ **Visit Faneuil Hall Marketplace**—restoration of Boston's historic Quincy Market. Shops, restaurants.

☐ **Go to the New England Aquarium**—412 species, 7,606 specimens.

☐ **Walk along the waterfront**—offices, shops, parks for picnics.

☐ **Take the "T"**—Boston's subway system.

☐ **Take a boat excursion**—cruise the harbor and Massachusetts Bay (1½ hours).

☐ **Go shopping in Downtown Crossing**—Boston's pedestrian zone.

☐ **Take an elevator to the top of the John Hancock Observatory**—the tallest building in New England.

☐ **Walk the Freedom Trail**—1½ miles of historic points of interest.

☐ **Eat at Legal Sea Foods**—restaurant chain famous for fresh fish at reasonable prices.

A: Wow, there's so much to do! I don't know where to begin!

B: Why don't we _____*visit Faneuil Hall Marketplace*_____? We can have
_{1.}

breakfast there and then do some shopping.

A: Sounds good. How will we get there?

B: Let's _____. I always like to see what
_{2.}

the public transportation is like.

A: OK. After that, maybe we could _____
_{3.}

and pick up some fresh fruit for later on. It's right across from there.

(continued)

B: We can't. It's only open Fridays and Saturdays.

A: Oh, too bad. How about _____ ?

4.

We could get a "bird's-eye" view of the city that way.

B: I don't know. I'm a little afraid of heights. But I've got another idea. Why don't we

_____ ? That way we could still see a

5.

lot of the city.

A: That sounds like a good idea. It'll be nice being on the water. And afterwards, how about

_____ ? I hear they have the largest

6.

glass-enclosed saltwater tank in the world.

B: Speaking of fish, why don't we _____

7.

tonight?

A: Good idea. But we should make a reservation. It's a very popular place.

B: So, we've decided what to do for breakfast and dinner. What about lunch?

A: Maybe we could _____ and have a

8.

picnic in the park.

B: And then, how about _____ ? I need to

9.

buy some souvenirs, and we won't have to worry about traffic. It's a pedestrian zone.

A: I don't know. Why don't we _____ ?

10.

I'd really like to see some more historic sights. We can look for souvenirs tomorrow.

4 | PERSONALIZATION

*Imagine you are in Boston with a friend. Look at the flyer in Exercise 3. Complete these
suggestions to your friend.*

1. Why don't we _____

2. How about _____

3. Let's _____

4. Maybe we could _____

5. But let's not _____

Present Perfect: *Since* and *For*

1 | SPELLING: REGULAR AND IRREGULAR VERBS

Write the past participles.

Base Form	Simple Past	Past Participle
1. be	was/were	*been*
2. bring	brought	_____
3. come	came	_____
4. eat	ate	_____
5. fall	fell	_____
6. get	got	_____
7. have	had	_____
8. look	looked	_____
9. lose	lost	_____
10. play	played	_____
11. watch	watched	_____
12. win	won	_____

2 | *SINCE* OR *FOR*

Complete these sentences with **since** *or* **for**.

1. I haven't known Ana ___*for*___ a long time.

2. She has been on my soccer team only _____ last September.

3. We've become good friends _____ then.

4. Our team hasn't been in a game _____ a few weeks.

5. _____ our last game, we've practiced a lot.

(continued)

77

6. _____ weeks we've gone to the field every day after class.

7. We haven't lost a game _____ several months.

8. I have loved sports _____ I was a little girl.

3 | AFFIRMATIVE STATEMENTS WITH *SINCE* AND *FOR*

Complete these biographies of two athletes who have been famous since they were children. Use the present perfect form of the verbs in parentheses and choose between **since** *and* **for**.

Biography A

Tiger Woods (1976–   ) When Tiger Woods was only 18 months old, his father gave him a sawed-off golf club. Woods ___*has loved*___
                                                                                                    1. (love)
the game of golf _____ then. As a teenager, he won
                  2. (since / for)
many amateur titles. At 16 he was the youngest person to play in a professional golf tournament.

_____ then, he _____ to win many
3. (Since / For)   **4. (go on)**
major tournaments and to break many records. _____ the past few years, TV
                                              5. (Since / For)
viewers _____ him in many commercials. _____ he turned
        6. (see)   **7. (Since / For)**
professional, Woods _____ more money and _____ more records
                    8. (earn)   **9. (break)**
at a younger age than any other golfer.

Biography B

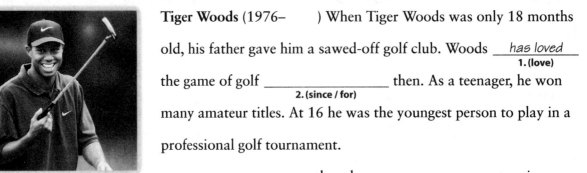

Michelle Kwan (1980–   ) Michelle Kwan _____ at
                                                            1. (be)
home on the ice _____ most of her life. She started
                2. (since / for)
skating when she was five and won her first skating competition a
year later. _____ that time, Kwan _____
            3. (Since / For)   **4. (win)**
more competitions—including five Worlds—than almost any other
skater, and she _____ one of the most famous figure
                5. (become)
skaters in the world. Her trophies include silver and bronze Olympic
medals, but not the gold—the prize she _____ of _____ she was a
                                        6. (dream)   **7. (since / for)**
little girl. _____ her last disappointment at the Olympics, Kwan _____
            8. (Since / For)   **9. (continue)**
skating, winning major competitions and thrilling audiences with her skill and grace.

4 | QUESTIONS AND ANSWERS

Use the words in parentheses to write questions about the athletes in Exercise 3. Look at the information again and answer the questions.

1. (How long / Tiger Woods / love golf)

   A: *How long has Tiger Woods loved golf?*

   B: *He has loved golf since he was 18 months old* OR *for more than 25 years.*

2. (How long / he / be a professional golfer)

   A: _____

   B: _____

3. (he / win any major tournaments since he turned professional)

   A: _____

   B: _____

4. (How long / he / be in TV commercials)

   A: _____

   B: _____

5. (How long / Michelle Kwan / be a skater)

   A: _____

   B: _____

6. (How many World Competitions / she / win since 1986)

   A: _____

   B: _____

7. (she / get an Olympic gold medal since she began competing)

   A: _____

   B: _____

8. (she / skate again since the Olympics)

   A: _____

   B: _____

5 | AFFIRMATIVE AND NEGATIVE STATEMENTS

Read each pair of sentences. Use the correct present perfect form to complete or write a summary sentence that has a meaning similar to the two sentences.

1. **a.** Tanya and Boris became skaters in 1998.

   b. They are still skaters.

   SUMMARY: _Tanya and Boris have been skaters_ _____ since 1998.

2. **a.** Fei-Mei and Natasha competed in 1992.

   b. That was the last time they competed.

   SUMMARY: _Fei-Mei and Natasha haven't competed since 1992._ _____

3. **a.** Min Ho won two awards in 1998.

   b. He won another award in 1999.

   SUMMARY: _____ since 1998.

4. **a.** Marilyn entered a competition in 1998.

   b. She entered another competition last year.

   SUMMARY: _____ since 1998.

5. **a.** Victor and Marilyn saw each other in 1998.

   b. That was the last time they saw each other.

   SUMMARY: _____

6. **a.** Karl became a golfer in 1999.

   b. He is still a golfer.

   SUMMARY: _____

7. **a.** Karl lost two tournaments in February of this year.

   b. He lost another tournament last week.

   SUMMARY: _____ since February of this year.

8. **a.** Andreas went to a tennis match two years ago.

   b. That was the last match he went to.

   SUMMARY: _____ for two years.

Present Perfect: *Already* and *Yet*

1 | SPELLING: REGULAR AND IRREGULAR VERBS

Write the past participles.

Base Form	Simple Past	Past Participle
1. act	acted	*acted*
2. become	became	_____
3. dance	danced	_____
4. drink	drank	_____
5. fight	fought	_____
6. give	gave	_____
7. hold	held	_____
8. keep	kept	_____
9. know	knew	_____
10. sing	sang	_____
11. smile	smiled	_____
12. travel	traveled	_____

2 | QUESTIONS AND STATEMENTS WITH *ALREADY* AND *YET*

*Complete this conversation with the correct form of the verbs in parentheses and **already** or **yet**. Choose between affirmative and negative. Use contractions if possible.*

TED: I hear you're looking for a new apartment. _____ *Have* _____ you

_____ *found* _____ one _____ *yet* _____?
      1. (find)

MIA: No. And we're getting discouraged. We _____ at more than 10, and
                                          2. (look)

we _____ one that we like _____!
      3. (find)

(continued)

TED: Well, don't give up. I _____ at least 20. Are you working with a
                                                   4. (see)

     real estate agent?

MIA: No. We wanted to try to find something ourselves, so we _____ to
                                                        5. (go)

     an agent _____. But I think we may need to. Unfortunately, we

     _____ a lot of time looking at apartments that were completely
                    6. (waste)
     wrong for us.

TED: I know what you mean. _____ you _____
                                                       7. (decide)

     on a neighborhood _____?

MIA: No. We _____ our minds _____. What
                        8. (make up)

     about you?

TED: We'd really like to stay in this neighborhood. We just need a bigger place.

3 | QUESTIONS AND STATEMENTS WITH *ALREADY* AND *YET*

*Mia is going to move. Read her list of things to do. She has checked (✓) all the things she's
already done. Write questions and answers about the words in parentheses.*

Moving Checklist

- ☑ choose a moving company
- ☐ find a painter
- ☑ collect boxes for packing
- ☑ get a change-of-address form from the post office
- ☐ begin to pack clothes
- ☑ make a list of cleaning supplies
- ☐ clean the refrigerator and stove
- ☑ buy two bookcases
- ☑ give away the old couch
- ☐ buy a new couch
- ☐ throw away old magazines
- ☐ invite the neighbors over for a good-bye party

1. **A:** (moving company) *Has she chosen a moving company yet?*

   B: *Yes, she's already chosen a moving company.*

2. **A:** (clothes) *Has she begun to pack clothes yet?*

   B: *No, she hasn't begun to pack clothes yet.*

3. **A:** (bookcases) _____

   B: _____

4. **A:** (magazines) _____

   B: _____

5. **A:** (painter) _____

   B: _____

6. **A:** (boxes) _____

   B: _____

7. **A:** (new couch) _____

   B: _____

8. **A:** (old couch) _____

   B: _____

9. **A:** (refrigerator and stove) _____

   B: _____

10. **A:** (cleaning supplies) _____

    B: _____

11. **A:** (change-of-address form) _____

    B: _____

12. **A:** (the neighbors) _____

    B: _____

4 | EDITING

*Mia sent an e-mail to her friend. There are six mistakes in the use of the present perfect with **already** and **yet**. The first one is already corrected. Find and correct five more.*

Hi,

    I'm writing to you from our new apartment! We've already ~~be~~ *been* here two weeks, and we feel very much at home. But there's still a lot to do. Believe it or not, we haven't unpacked all the boxes already! We took most of our old furniture, so we don't need to get too much new stuff. We had to buy a new couch for the living room, but they haven't delivered it yet.

    We've already meet some of our new neighbors. They seem very nice. One of them have already invited us over for coffee.

    Had you made vacation plans yet? As soon as we get the couch (it's a sleeper), we'd love for you to visit. Already we've planned places to take you when you come!

—Mia

Present Perfect: Indefinite Past

1 | SPELLING: REGULAR AND IRREGULAR VERBS

Write the past participles.

Base Form	Simple Past	Past Participle
1. begin	began	*begun*
2. decide	decided	_____
3. fly	flew	_____
4. go	went	_____
5. hear	heard	_____
6. keep	kept	_____
7. make	made	_____
8. ride	rode	_____
9. see	saw	_____
10. swim	swam	_____
11. travel	traveled	_____
12. work	worked	_____

2 | AFFIRMATIVE STATEMENTS

Complete these statements. Use the present perfect form of the correct verbs from Exercise 1.

1. Julie _____ *has made* _____ several trips this year.

2. You _____ on a camel. Did you enjoy it?

3. I'd like to go to Costa Rica. I _____ that it's beautiful.

4. They _____ the Pyramids before.

5. He _____ Air France many times. It's his favorite airline.

(continued)

6. I _____ with dolphins in the ocean. What an adventure!

7. My cousin _____ to go hiking in northern Spain next fall.

8. She _____ hard this year and really needs a vacation.

3 | AFFIRMATIVE AND NEGATIVE STATEMENTS

Read this article about a famous series of travel guides. Complete the sentences with the present perfect form of the verbs in parentheses.

As you probably know, travel _____*has become*_____ very, very popular. As a result,
        1. (become)

hundreds of travel guides _____ on bookstore shelves. One of the most
       2. (appear)

popular travel-guide series is *Lonely Planet*. It began in the early 1970s by Tony and Maureen

Wheeler. The husband-and-wife team _____ always really

_____ traveling, and they _____. They still make
    3. (love)   **4. (not stop)**

a lot of trips all over the world. The first *Lonely Planet* guidebook was the result of one of their

first trips. Today the series has more than 650 guidebooks, and Tony Wheeler

_____ and _____ to more than 20 of them. The
      5. (write)   **6. (contribute)**

Wheelers _____ both _____ awards for their
                   7. (receive)

work, and *The New York Times* _____ Tony as "the most influential man
              8. (describe)

in travel."

Recently, *Lonely Planet* _____ a new edition of all their books. The
           9. (introduce)

publisher _____ almost 4,000 new maps and 23,000 new pages. Tony
     10. (include)

Wheeler says this "re-launch" _____ them a real opportunity to improve
           11. (give)

the series. The huge project _____ easy, but according to publisher Simon
         12. (not be)

Westcott, it _____ worth the effort. "We're really proud of what we
     13. (be)

_____," he said. "We _____ the best guidebooks
   14. (do)   **15. (produce)**

a traveler can buy."

Lonely Planet books are quite different from other guidebooks. The travel series

_____ always _____ travelers to do and explore
              16. (encourage)

new things—not just the "Top-Ten Tourist Sights." If you _____ a *Lonely*
              17. (not read)

Planet guide, check one out. We promise you: It will be an adventure—even if you never leave

your armchair!

4 | QUESTIONS AND ANSWERS WITH ADVERBS AND TIME EXPRESSIONS

A travel agent is talking to a client. Complete the travel agent's questions with the words in parentheses. Use the agent's notes and the correct adverb or time expression from the box to answer the questions. You will use some words more than once.

many times	never	not lately	once	recently	twice

Adventure Travel Inc.

Egypt— 2 X
Europe— more than 10 X
African safari— (returned two months ago)
Costa Rica—1 X (1999)
China— no

hot-air ballooning— no
dolphin swim— 6 X or more

group tour— no (and <u>not</u> interested)

---

1. **AGENT:** <u>Have you ever been</u> _____ to Egypt?
   (ever / be)

   CLIENT: <u>I've been to Egypt twice.</u> _____

2. **AGENT:** _____ Europe?
   (How many times / visit)

   CLIENT: _____

3. **AGENT:** _____ on an African safari?
   (ever / be)

   CLIENT: _____

4. **AGENT:** _____ to Costa Rica?
   (ever / be)

   CLIENT: _____

5. **AGENT:** _____ there?
   (How often / be)

   CLIENT: _____

(continued)

6. **AGENT:** _____ in China?
   (travel)

   CLIENT: _____

7. **AGENT:** _____ in a hot-air balloon?
   (ever / go up)

   CLIENT: _____

8. **AGENT:** _____ with dolphins?
   (ever / swim)

   CLIENT: _____

9. **AGENT:** _____ a group tour?
   (ever / take)

   CLIENT: _____ . And I never want to!

5 | PERSONALIZATION

Write sentences about your own travel experience. Use the present perfect with adverbs or time expressions like **never**, **twice**, **recently**, **not lately**, *and* **many times**.

1. _____

2. _____

3. _____

4. _____

5. _____

6. _____

Present Perfect and Simple Past

1 | PRESENT PERFECT OR SIMPLE PAST

Complete the sentences about Tom Dorsey, a teacher who is looking for a job in another city.

Last Year

1. Tom answered 20 employment ads.

2. _____ Tom had _____ two job interviews.

3. Tom went on one out-of-town interview.

4. _____ one job offer.

5. Tom made $30,000.

6. _____ a lot of interesting people.

7. Tom was sick once.

8. _____ well.

9. _____ a new camera.

10. Tom paid with cash.

11. Tom read five books.

12. Tom didn't take a vacation.

13. Tom didn't give any parties.

14. _____ discouraged.

This Year

_____ Tom has answered _____ 30 ads.

Tom has had three job interviews.

_____ on two out-of-town interviews.

Tom has gotten three job offers.

_____ the same amount of money.

Tom has met a lot of interesting people too.

_____ sick twice.

Tom has looked tired.

Tom has bought a DVD player.

_____ by credit card.

_____ two books.

_____ a vacation. He went to Florida.

_____ two parties.

Tom has felt more encouraged.

2 | PRESENT PERFECT OR SIMPLE PAST

A journalist is interviewing a woman about marriage. Complete the interview with the correct form of the verbs in parentheses. Use the present perfect or the simple past.

INTERVIEWER: How long _____*have*_____ you _____*been*_____ married?
                                              1. (be)

WOMAN: We _____ married in 2001, so we _____ married for
              2. (get)   **3. (be)**
just a few years.

INTERVIEWER: And when _____ you _____ your first child?
                                                    4. (have)

WOMAN: Well, I _____ a mother pretty quickly. We _____
                5. (become)   **6. (have)**
Stephanie 10 months after we _____ married.
                                      7. (be)

INTERVIEWER: You say this isn't your first marriage. How long _____ your first
marriage _____?
              8. (last)

WOMAN: About two years. We _____ in 1998.
                                    9. (divorce)

INTERVIEWER: _____ the two of you _____ any kids?
                                                10. (have)

WOMAN: No, we _____.
                        11.

INTERVIEWER: Do you still see your first husband?

WOMAN: Yes. We _____ friends. In fact, I _____ him last week.
                12. (remain)   **13. (see)**
He and Tom _____ friends too.
                14. (become)

INTERVIEWER: _____ he _____?
                                      15. (remarry)

WOMAN: No, he _____.
                        16.

INTERVIEWER: In your opinion, why _____ your first marriage _____?
                                                                          17. (fail)

WOMAN: I think that we _____ married too young. We _____
                        18. (get)   **19. (not know)**
each other well enough.

INTERVIEWER: Where _____ you _____ Tom?
                                          20. (meet)

WOMAN: In Atlanta. We _____ both students there.
                        21. (be)

INTERVIEWER: And when _____ you _____ to Los Angeles?
                                                    22. (move)

WOMAN: Last year. Los Angeles is the third city we _____ in! Tom is a college
                                                          23. (live)
professor, and it's hard to find a permanent job these days.

3 | PRESENT PERFECT OR SIMPLE PAST

Read some facts about the changing American family. Complete the sentences with the present perfect or simple past form of the verbs in the boxes.

begin	~~change~~	get	have

The American family ____has changed____ a lot in the past 45 years. In the 1960s, couples
          1.
_____ to get married at an older age. They also _____ divorced more
   2.   **3.**
frequently than they ever did, and they _____ fewer children.
                                          4.

be	create	occur	rise

Age

In 1960, the average age for marriage for women _____ 20.3 and for men,
                                          5.
22.8. Today it _____ to 25.1 for women and 26.8 for men. In the early 1960s, most
        6.
divorces _____ among couples older than 45. Today people of all ages are getting
      7.
divorced at a very high rate. This, in part, _____ many single-parent homes.
                                   8.

be	have	increase	start

Birth Rate

In the mid-1960s, birth rates _____ to drop. Then, almost 60 percent of women
                          9.
_____ three or more children by the time they _____ in their late 30s.
   10.   **11.**
These days, 35 percent of women in the same age group have only two children. In addition, the
number of births to older women _____ greatly _____.
                                                  12.

change	get	reach	stay

Living Arrangements

Before 1960, most children _____ in their parents' homes until they
                               13.
_____ married. This pattern _____ since then. Today many single
   14.   **15.**

(continued)

people live alone. Also affecting today's living arrangements is the fact that life expectancy

_____ an all-time high of 77.6 years. This means that there are a lot more older
  16.

people, and some of them are moving in with their adult children.

4 | EDITING

*Read this student's e-mail to a friend. There are eight mistakes in the use of the present perfect
and the simple past. The first mistake is already corrected. Find and correct seven more.*

Hi, Jennifer—

            met
Last month, I ~~have met~~ the most wonderful guy. His name is Roger, and he is a

student in my night class. He lived here since 1992. Before that he lived in Detroit

too, so we have a lot in common. Roger has been married for five years but got

divorced last April.

    Roger and I spent a lot of time together. Last week I saw him every night, and this

week we already gotten together three times after class. Monday night we have

seen a great movie. Did you see *The Purple Room*? It's playing at all the theaters.

    We've decided to take a trip back to Detroit in the summer. Maybe we can get

together. It would be great to see you again. Please let me know if you'll be there.

Love,

Diana

Here's a photo of Roger that I've taken a few weeks ago.

5 | PERSONALIZATION

Complete these sentences with information about your own life.

1. This year, _____

2. Last year, _____

3. _____ since 2000.

4. Four years ago, _____

5. For the past two years, _____

20 Present Perfect Progressive and Present Perfect

1 | PRESENT PERFECT PROGRESSIVE STATEMENTS

Read the information about Amanda and Pete Kelly. Write a sentence—affirmative or negative—that summarizes the information. Use the present perfect progressive with **since** *or* **for**.

1. It's 9:00. Amanda began working at 7:00. She is still working.

   Amanda has been working since 7:00 OR for two hours.

2. She is writing articles about elephants. She began a series last month.

   _____

3. Amanda and Pete used to live in New York. They left New York a few years ago.

   _____

4. They are now living in London. They moved there in 2004.

   _____

5. Pete was selling books. He stopped last year.

   _____

6. Pete and Amanda are thinking of opening their own business. They began thinking about this last year.

   _____

7. Pete went back to school last month. He's studying economics.

   _____

8. Amanda and Pete started looking for a new apartment a month ago. They're still looking.

   _____

2 | PRESENT PERFECT PROGRESSIVE OR PRESENT PERFECT

Read this article about a famous British businesswoman and environmentalist. Complete the information with the present perfect progressive or present perfect form of the verbs in parentheses. If both forms are possible, use the present perfect progressive.

Born in 1942, the child of an Italian immigrant family living in England, Anita Roddick _____ *has become* _____ one of the
                                                    1. (become)
most successful businesswomen in the world. Today she is the owner of an international chain of stores that sells soaps, makeup, body lotions, and creams. For more than 25 years, The Body Shop

_____ products that are "environmentally
        2. (sell)
friendly." They are made mostly of natural products from renewable sources, and they come in biodegradable, recyclable containers. In addition, Roddick, who _____
                                                                    3. (fight)
for years against the practice of animal testing of cosmetics, refuses to use any animals to test her products.

The first Body Shop opened in Brighton, England, in 1976. Since then, more than 2,000 stores in 50 countries around the world _____.
                                                    4. (open)
Roddick relies on the reputation of her products and stores to attract customers. She

_____ never _____ much advertising for her
                                        5. (do)
stores. Word of mouth _____ her chief way of getting new customers.
                                6. (be)
Roddick spends much of her time traveling. Right now she is "on the road." For the past several months, she _____ around the world in search of new ideas for
                                7. (travel)
her body-care products.

Roddick is more than a businesswoman. She _____ several awards,
                                                        8. (receive)
including the United Nations Global 500 environmental award. She is also concerned with human rights. Lately, she _____ hard to improve the earnings of workers who
                                        9. (work)
make clothes for large multinational stores.

(continued)

Roddick _____ several books. Her latest one, *Business as Unusual:*

10. (write)

My Entrepreneurial Journey, tells how Roddick _____ successfully

_____ business with social responsibility. She hopes her story will serve as

11. (combine)

a model to other people. According to one writer for *Inc.*, a business magazine, it already has:

"This woman _____ business forever," wrote Bo Burlingham in 1990.

12. (change)

More than 15 years later, Roddick continues to be a force for change in both the business and

social worlds.

3 | PRESENT PERFECT PROGRESSIVE OR PRESENT PERFECT

*Complete this conversation between two friends. Use the present perfect progressive or
present perfect form of the verbs in parentheses.*

A: Hi. I _____*haven't seen*_____ you around lately. How _____

1. (not see)

you _____?

2. (be)

B: OK, thanks. What about you?

A: Not bad. What _____ you _____?

3. (do)

B: Nothing special. What about you?

A: I _____ a book for this business course I'm taking. It's called *Business*

4. (read)

as Unusual. It's pretty interesting.

B: Who wrote it?

A: Anita Roddick. _____ you ever _____

5. (read)

anything about her?

B: Yes. I _____ a few articles about her in the paper.

6. (see)

A: _____ you ever _____ any of her products?

7. (buy)

B: As a matter of fact, I _____ her products for years.

8. (use)

A: Oh. Where do you buy them?

B: I used to go downtown, but a new Body Shop _____ just

_____ on Broadway.

9. (open)

A: Wow, they _____ everywhere, haven't they? I wonder where the next

10. (open)

one is going to be.

4 | QUESTIONS: PRESENT PERFECT PROGRESSIVE OR PRESENT PERFECT

Write questions about Anita Roddick. Use the words in parentheses and the present perfect progressive or present perfect.

1. (she / sell / body products for a long time)

   Has she been selling body products for a long time?

2. (How long / she / be / a businesswoman)

3. (How much money / her business / make this year)

4. (How long / she / travel around the world)

5. (How many countries / she / visit)

6. (her shops / open / in Asia)

7. (How many copies of her book / she / sell)

8. (she / write / any books since *Business as Unusual*)

9. (How many awards / she / receive)

10. (What / she / work on / these days)

11. (How long / she and her husband / live in England)

5 | EDITING

Read this journal entry. There are seven mistakes in the use of the present perfect progressive and present perfect. The first mistake is already corrected. Find and correct six more.

Friday, Sept. 15

                              been taking

It's the second week of the fall semester. I've ~~taken~~ a business course with Professor

McCarthy. For the past two weeks, we've studying people who have been becoming very

successful in the world of business. As part of the course, we've been reading books by

or about internationally famous businesspeople.

    For example, I've just been finishing a book by Bill Gates, the CEO of Microsoft,

called Business @ the Speed of Thought. It was fascinating. Since then, I've read

Business as Unusual by Anita Roddick, the owner of The Body Shop. I've only been

reading about 50 pages of the book so far, but it seems interesting. Although I bought

her products ever since one of her stores opened in my neighborhood, I really didn't

know much about her.

Nouns and Quantifiers

1 | KINDS OF NOUNS

Write each noun in the correct column.

~~bottle~~	chair	Chirac	class	country	cup
December	euro	furniture	garden	hamburger	history
honesty	ink	Korean	money	month	news
oil	pen	president	rice	snow	snowflake
spaghetti	story	sugar	swimming	Todd	water

Proper Nouns	Common Nouns	
	Count	Non-count
_____	*bottle*	_____
_____	_____	_____
_____	_____	_____
_____	_____	_____
	_____	_____
	_____	_____
	_____	_____
	_____	_____
	_____	_____
	_____	_____
	_____	_____
	_____	_____

2 | COUNT AND NON-COUNT NOUNS

Read these food facts. Complete the sentences with the correct form of the words in parentheses.

1. ___Chocolate___ ___has___ a chemical that creates a feeling similar to being in love.
   (Chocolate) (have)

2. _____ _____ the most popular food in the United States.
   (Potato) (be)

   _____ _____ the most popular food in the world.
   (Rice) (be)

3. _____ _____ Americans' favorite snack food. _____
   (Potato chip) (be) (American)

   _____ more potato chips than any other _____ in the world.
   (eat) (people)

4. Chewing raw onions for five minutes _____ all the germs in your mouth.
   (kill)

5. _____ _____ at least 5,000 years old.
   (Popcorn) (be)

6. _____ _____ really nuts. They are members of the bean family.
   (Peanut) (not be)

7. _____ _____ been around for just a little over 100 years. It's a relatively
   (Peanut butter) (have)
   new food product.

8. The _____ of the hot dog _____ very long. It began 3,500 years ago.
   (history) (be)

9. _____ _____ the favorite dessert in the United States.
   (Ice cream) (be)

   _____ _____ the two favorite flavors.
   (Vanilla and chocolate) (be)

3 | MUCH OR MANY

*Complete this food quiz. Use **much** or **many**. Then try to guess the answer to the questions. Circle the letter of your choice. (You can find the answers to the quiz on page AK-15.)*

1. How ___much___ vitamin C does an onion have? As ___much___ as . . .

   a. two apples
   b. one orange
   c. three carrots

2. How _____ rolls are there in a "baker's dozen"?

   a. eleven
   b. twelve
   c. thirteen

3. How _____ pizza does the average person from the United States eat each year?

   a. 13 pounds
   b. 23 pounds
   c. 33 pounds

4. In how _____ countries can you find a McDonald's fast-food restaurant?

   a. almost 50
   b. almost 80
   c. almost 120

5. How _____ chocolate does the average person in Switzerland eat each year?

   a. 10.7 pounds
   b. 20.7 pounds
   c. 30.7 pounds

6. How _____ calories are there in a cup of regular vanilla ice cream?

   a. 170
   b. 270
   c. 370

7. How _____ ice cream does the average person in Finland eat each year?

   a. 22 pints
   b. 38 pints
   c. 46 pints

8. How _____ weeks is it safe to keep butter in the refrigerator?

   a. four
   b. six
   c. eight

4 | QUANTIFIERS

Some people are talking at a neighborhood block party. Read the conversations and circle the correct words.

1. **A:** Hi. I'm Carmen Del Rey. I've seen you walking your dog much /(a few) times.
   a.

   B: I'm Jim Terrell. I just moved here. I don't know many / much people yet.
   b.

   A: I'll introduce you to a little / a few neighbors. Everyone is very friendly here.
   c.

2. **A:** There's a lot of / many food!
   a.

   B: I know. Everybody brought any / some. Try a little /a few potato salad. It's delicious.
   b.   **c.**

   A: Thanks, but I want to save enough / any room for dessert.
   d.

(continued)

3. **A:** I don't see <u>some / many</u> kids. Are there <u>any / a little</u> families with children?
           a.   **b.**

   B: There are <u>several / much</u>. The kids are probably all in the Guptas' backyard. They have a
                      c.

     pool and <u>many / a lot of</u> play equipment.
              d.

4. **A:** It's nice to see everyone. We don't spend <u>enough / many</u> time together.
                                       a.

   B: I know. We're all so busy and have <u>a little / little</u> free time.
                                     b.

5 | PERSONALIZATION

Describe a party or another social event you've attended. Who was there? What kind of food did they have at the event?

_____

_____

_____

_____

_____

Articles: Indefinite and Definite

1 | INDEFINITE AND DEFINITE ARTICLES

Some people are talking in school. Choose the correct word to complete the conversations.
If you don't need an article, circle Ø.

1. **A:** Can I borrow (a) / the pen?

   B: Sure. Take a / the one on a / the desk. I don't need it.

2. **A:** Is a / the teacher here yet?

   B: No, she hasn't come yet.

3. **A:** What do you think of Mr. Mencz?

   B: He's a / the best teacher I've ever had.

4. **A:** Have you done the / Ø homework?

   B: Yes. But I don't think I got a / the last answer right.

5. **A:** Could you open a / the window, please?

   B: Which one?

   A: A / The one next to a / the door.

6. **A:** Who's that?

   B: That's a / the school principal.

   A: Oh, I've never seen her before.

7. **A:** Do you like the / Ø history?

   B: It's OK. But I prefer the / Ø science. What about you?

   A: I'm very interested in a / the history of the / Ø ancient Greece.

8. **A:** We learned about an / the ozone layer in science class yesterday.

   B: Did you know there's a / the hole in it?

   A: Yeah. It's pretty scary.

(continued)

9. **A:** What kind of work do you do?

   B: I'm <u>an / the</u> engineer. What about you?

   A: I'm <u>a / Ø</u> mechanic.

10. **A:** Are they <u>some / Ø</u> students?

    B: I don't think so. They look like <u>the / Ø</u> teachers.

11. **A:** Do you know where I can get <u>some / the</u> water around here?

    B: Sure. There's <u>a / the</u> water fountain right across <u>a / the</u> hall, right next to <u>the / Ø</u> restrooms.

12. **A:** Do you know what <u>a / the</u> homework is for tomorrow?

    B: We have to read <u>a / the</u> fable.

    A: Which one?

    B: <u>A / The</u> one on page 23.

2 | INDEFINITE AND DEFINITE ARTICLES

Complete the conversation. Use **a / an** *or* **the** *where necessary. Leave a blank if you don't need an article.*

BING YANG: Hi, Georgina. What are you doing?

GEORGINA: I'm reading ____*a*____ fable for my English class.
　　　　　　　　　　　　　　　1.

BING YANG: What's _____ fable? I've never heard _____ word before.
　　　　　　　　　　　　　2.　　　　　　　　　　　　　3.

GEORGINA: _____ fable is _____ short story about _____ animals.
　　　　　　　　4.　　　　　　　5.　　　　　　　　　　　6.

BING YANG: About _____ animals? Like _____ science story?
　　　　　　　　　　　　7.　　　　　　　　　8.

GEORGINA: No. It's _____ fiction. _____ animals act like _____ people. They
　　　　　　　　　　　　9.　　　　　　　10.　　　　　　　　　11.

　　　　　　　　usually teach _____ lesson. _____ lesson is called _____ moral of
　　　　　　　　　　　　　12.　　　　　　　13.　　　　　　　　　14.

　　　　　　　　_____ story, and it always comes at _____ end.
　　　　　　　　15.　　　　　　　　　　　　　　　16.

BING YANG: That's interesting. Who's _____ author of _____ fable you're reading?
　　　　　　　　　　　　　　　　　17.　　　　　　　18.

GEORGINA: Aesop. He was _____ ancient Greek writer.
　　　　　　　　　　　　　19.

BING YANG: Oh, now I know what you're talking about. My parents used to read _____
　　　　　　　　　　　　　　　　　　　　　　　　　　　　　　　　　　　20.

　　　　　　　　fables to me when I was _____ child.
　　　　　　　　　　　　　　　　21.

GEORGINA: Well, they're also good for _____ adults. I'll lend you _____ book when I'm
　　　　　　　　　　　　　　　　　　　22.　　　　　　　　　23.

　　　　　　　　finished if you're interested.

BING YANG: Thanks. I am.

3 | INDEFINITE AND DEFINITE ARTICLES

Complete this version of an Aesop fable. Use **a / an** *or* **the** *where necessary. Leave a blank if you don't need an article.*

The Fox and the Goat

____A____ fox fell into _____ well and
    1.   **2.**

couldn't get out again. Finally, _____ thirsty goat
                                3.

came by and saw _____ fox in _____ well. "Is
                  4.   **5.**

_____ water good?" _____ goat asked.
   6.   **7.**

"Good?" asked _____ fox. "It's _____ best
                 8.   **9.**

water I've ever tasted in my whole life. Why don't you

come down and try it?"

_____ goat was very thirsty, so he jumped into
  10.

_____ well. When he was finished drinking, he looked for _____ way to get out of
 11.   **12.**

_____ well, but, of course, there wasn't any. Then _____ fox said, "I have _____
 13.   **14.**   **15.**

excellent idea. Stand on your back legs and place your front legs firmly against _____ front
                                                          16.

side of _____ well. Then, I'll climb onto your back and, from there, I'll step on your horns
       17.

and I'll be able to get out. When I'm out, I'll help you get out too." _____ goat thought this
                                                        18.

was _____ good idea and followed _____ advice.
   19.   **20.**

When _____ fox was out of _____ well, he quickly and quietly walked away.
        21.   **22.**

_____ goat called loudly after him and reminded him of _____ promise he had made to
 23.   **24.**

help him out. But _____ fox turned and said, "You should have as much sense in your head
             25.

as you have _____ hairs in your beard. You jumped into _____ well before making sure
          26.   **27.**

you could get out again."

MORAL: *Look before you leap.*

4 | INDEFINITE AND DEFINITE ARTICLES

Complete this student's essay. Use **a / an** *or* **the** *where necessary. Leave a blank if you don't need an article.*

_____A_____ fox is _____ member of
   1.   **2.**

_____ dog family. It looks like _____
   3.   **4.**

small, thin dog with _____ bushy tail,
                        5.

_____ long nose, and _____ pointed
   6.   **7.**

ears. You can find _____ foxes in most
                       8.

parts of _____ world. _____ animal moves very fast, and it is
            9.   **10.**

_____ very good hunter. It eats mostly _____ mice, but it also eats
   11.   **12.**

_____ birds, insects, rabbits, and fruit.
   13.

   Unfortunately, _____ people hunt _____ foxes for their beautiful
                      14.   **15.**

fur. They also hunt them for another reason. _____ fox is _____
                                                16.   **17.**

intelligent, clever animal, and this makes it hard to catch. As _____
                                                                   18.

result, _____ hunters find it exciting to try to catch one. It is also
           19.

because of its cleverness that _____ fox often appears in _____
                                  20.   **21.**

fables such as _____ fable we just read in class.
                  22.

Adjectives and Adverbs

1 | SPELLING

Write the adjectives and adverbs.

Adjectives	Adverbs
1. quick	*quickly*
2. _____	nicely
3. fast	_____
4. good	_____
5. _____	dangerously
6. beautiful	_____
7. _____	hard
8. safe	_____
9. _____	occasionally
10. _____	happily
11. _____	suddenly
12. careful	_____
13. angry	_____
14. _____	unfortunately
15. bad	_____
16. _____	thoughtfully
17. _____	hungrily
18. extreme	_____

2 WORD ORDER

Emily is telling her friend about her new apartment. Unscramble the words to complete the conversation.

Anna: Congratulations! <u>I heard about your new apartment</u>   .
1. (heard about / I / apartment / new / your)

Emily: Thank you! _____ !
2. (news / good / fast / travels)

Anna: What's it like?

Emily: _____ ,
3. (five / rooms / has / it / large)

_____ ,
4. (building / it's / large / a / very / in)

and _____ .
5. (sunny / it's / very)

Anna: How's the rent?

Emily: _____ .
6. (too / it's / bad / not)

Anna: And what about the neighborhood?

Emily: _____ .
7. (seems / quiet / it / pretty)

But _____ .
8. (landlord / the / very / speaks / loudly)

Anna: How come?

Emily: _____ .
9. (well / doesn't / he / hear)

Anna: Well, that doesn't really matter. _____ ?
10. (it / decision / was / hard / a)

Emily: No. Not really. We really liked the apartment a lot, and besides,

_____ .
11. (quickly / had to / we / decide)

There were a lot of other people interested in it.

Anna: Oh, no! Look at the time! _____ .
12. (I / leave / now / have to)

_____ !
13. (luck / with / good / apartment / new / your)

Emily: Thanks. See you soon.

3 | ADJECTIVE OR ADVERB

Emily wrote a letter to a friend. Complete the letter with the correct form of the words in parentheses.

Dear Lauren,

I'm _____totally_____ exhausted! James and I finished moving into our
      1. (total)

new apartment today. It was a lot of _____ work, but everything
                                        2. (hard)

worked out _____.
              3. (good)

   The apartment looks very _____. It's _____
                               4. (nice)   **5. (extreme)**

_____. The only problem is with the heat. It seems that I always
6. (comfortable)

feel _____. We'll have to speak to the landlord about it. He seems
      7. (cold)

_____ _____.
   8. (pretty)   **9. (friendly)**

   People tell me that the neighborhood is very _____. That's
                                                   10. (safe)

_____ _____ because, as you know, I get home pretty
   11. (real)   **12. (important)**

_____ from work. I hate it when the streets are _____
   13. (late)   **14. (complete)**

_____ like they were in our old neighborhood. Shopping is very
   15. (empty)

_____, too. We can get to all the stores very _____.
   16. (good)   **17. (easy)**

The bus stop is _____ the apartment, and all of the buses run
                   18. (near)

_____. Everything is _____ and _____.
   19. (frequent)   **20. (nice)**   **21. (convenient)**

   Why don't you come for a visit? It would be _____ to see you.
                                                  22. (wonderful)

I haven't seen you since our wedding. Please write.

                                             Love,

                                             Emily

P.S. I almost _____ forgot to tell you! James got a _____
                23. (complete)   **24. (new)**

job as a computer programmer. He feels _____ _____
                                          25. (real)   **26. (happy)**

about it, and that, of course, makes me _____ too.
                                           27. (happy)

4 | -ED OR -ING ADJECTIVES

Emily and James are going to rent a DVD. Circle the correct adjective form to complete these brief movie reviews.

At Home at the Movies

BILLY BUDD Based on Herman Melville's powerful and (**1.** fascinated / fascinating) novel, this well-acted, well-produced film will leave you (**2.** disturbed / disturbing).

THE BURNING There's nothing at all (**3.** entertained / entertaining) about this 1981 horror film that takes place in a summer camp. You'll be (**4.** disgusted / disgusting) by all the blood in this story of revenge.

CHARIOTS OF FIRE Made in England, this is an (**5.** inspired / inspiring) story about two Olympic runners. Wonderfully acted.

COMING HOME Jon Voight plays the role of a (**6.** paralyzed / paralyzing) war veteran in this (**7.** moved / moving) drama about the effects of war. Powerful.

THE COMPETITION Well-acted love story about two pianists who fall in love while competing for the top prize in a music competition. You'll be (**8.** moved / moving). Beautiful music.

FOLLOW ME QUIETLY An extraordinarily (**9.** frightened / frightening) thriller about a mentally (**10.** disturbed / disturbing) man who kills people when it rains. Not for the weak-hearted.

THE GRADUATE Director Mike Nichols won an Academy Award for this funny but (**11.** touched / touching) look at a young man trying to figure out his life after college.

THE GREEN WALL Mario Robles Godoy's photography is absolutely (**12.** astonished / astonishing) in this story of a young Peruvian family. In Spanish with English subtitles.

INVASION OF THE BODY SNATCHERS One of the most (**13.** frightened / frightening) science-fiction movies ever made. You won't be (**14.** bored / boring).

WEST SIDE STORY No matter how many times you see this classic musical, you will never be (**15.** disappointed / disappointing). The story, based on Shakespeare's *Romeo and Juliet*, is (**16.** touched / touching), and the music by Leonard Bernstein is delightful and (**17.** excited / exciting).

WILBUR AND ORVILLE: THE FIRST TO FLY This is an exceptionally (**18.** entertained / entertaining) biography of the two famous Wright brothers. Good for kids too. They'll learn a lot without ever being (**19.** bored / boring).

Adjectives: Comparisons with *As . . . as* and *Than*

1 | SPELLING: REGULAR AND IRREGULAR COMPARATIVES

Write the comparative forms of the adjectives.

Adjective	Comparative
1. amazing	*more amazing*
2. bad	
3. big	
4. careful	
5. cheap	
6. comfortable	
7. dangerous	
8. difficult	
9. early	
10. expensive	
11. far	
12. good	
13. hot	
14. long	
15. noisy	
16. pretty	
17. slow	
18. terrible	
19. wet	
20. wide	

2 | COMPARISONS WITH AS . . .AS

Look at the information comparing two pizza restaurants. Complete the sentences with
just as . . . as *or* **not as . . . as** *and the correct form of the words in parentheses.*

	PIZZA PALACE	JOE'S PIZZERIA
Year opened	1990	1990
Number of tables	40	20
Pizza size	12 inches	12 inches
Price of a cheese pizza	$8.00	$8.00
Choice of pizza toppings	15	7
Average waiting time for a table	10 minutes	5 minutes
Hours	noon–11:00 P.M. (7 days a week)	noon–8:00 P.M. (closed Mondays)
Atmosphere	★★	★
Service	★★	★★
Cleanliness	★★	★★
Food	★★	★★★

1. The Pizza Palace is _____*just as old as*_____ Joe's Pizzeria.
   (old)

2. Joe's is _____ the Pizza Palace.
   (large)

3. A pizza from Joe's is _____ one from the Pizza Palace.
   (big)

4. The pizza at the Pizza Palace is _____ the pizza at Joe's.
   (expensive)

5. The choice of toppings at Joe's is _____ the choice at the Pizza
   (varied)

   Palace.

6. The waiting time at Joe's is _____ it is at the Pizza Palace.
   (long)

7. The hours at Joe's are _____ the hours at the Pizza Palace.
   (convenient)

8. Closing hour at Joe's is _____ it is at the Pizza Palace.
   (late)

9. The atmosphere at Joe's is _____ it is at the Pizza Palace.
   (nice)

10. The service at Joe's is _____ the service at the Pizza Palace.
    (good)

11. The pizza at the Pizza Palace is _____ it is at Joe's.
    (good)

12. Joe's is _____ the Pizza Palace.
    (clean)

3 | COMPARATIVES WITH *THAN*

These conversations took place at the Pizza Palace. Complete the sentences with the correct form of the adjectives in parentheses. Use **than** *when necessary.*

1. **A:** Wow, this place has gotten really popular!

   B: I know. It's even _____*more popular than*_____ Joe's.
   (popular)

2. **A:** I can't believe how long the line is!

   B: Maybe we should come for an _____ dinner next time.
   (early)

3. **A:** I prefer that table over there.

   B: Me too. It looks _____.
   (comfortable)

4. **A:** Let's order pizza number 7—with spinach and tomatoes.

   B: OK. That sounds _____ the one with pepperoni and extra cheese.
   (healthy)

5. **A:** This pizza is great.

   B: It *is* good, but I still think the pizza at Joe's is _____ the
   (good)

   pizza here.

6. **A:** Do you want to go to a movie after dinner? We could see *Crash*.

   B: Let's see *Star Wars 3*. It's _____.
   (exciting)

7. **A:** Hey, is that Brian over there at that table?

   B: No. Brian is much _____ that guy.
   (tall)

8. **A:** It sure is noisy in here.

   B: I know. But it's _____ Joe's!
   (quiet)

9. **A:** I bet the noise here is _____ on weekends.
   (bad)

   B: I'm sure it is.

10. **A:** It's already 8:00.

    B: Oh! I thought it was _____ that.
    (late)

11. **A:** Do you ever make pizza yourself?

    B: No. I buy it frozen. It's _____ just to pop it in the microwave.
    (fast)

12. **A:** I really should buy a microwave oven.

    B: You really should. It will make your life _____.
    (easy)

4 | COMPARATIVES WITH *THAN*

*Look at this chart comparing two microwave ovens. Complete the sentences with the appropriate comparative form of the adjectives in parentheses and **than**. Also, fill in the blanks with the brand—**X** or **Y**.*

Brand	Price	Size (cubic ft.)	Weight (lbs.)	Defrosting	Heating	Speed	Noise
X	$181	0.5	31	●	○	◒	○
Y	$147	0.6	36	◒	●	●	◒

1. Brand ____X____ is ___*more expensive than*___ Brand ___Y___.
                                (expensive)

2. Brand _____ is _____ Brand _____.
                              (cheap)

3. Brand _____ is _____ Brand _____.
                              (large)

4. Brand _____ is _____ Brand _____.
                              (small)

5. Brand _____ is _____ Brand _____.
                              (heavy)

6. Brand _____ is _____ Brand _____.
                              (light)

7. For defrosting food, Brand _____ is _____ Brand _____.
                                                (efficient)

8. For heating food, Brand _____ is _____ Brand _____.
                                              (effective)

9. Brand _____ is _____ Brand _____.
                              (fast)

10. Brand _____ is _____ Brand _____.
                              (slow)

11. Brand _____ is _____ Brand _____.
                              (noisy)

12. Brand _____ is _____ Brand _____.
                              (quiet)

13. In general, Brand _____ seems _____ Brand _____.
                                            (good)

14. In general, Brand _____ seems _____ Brand _____.
                                            (bad)

5 | COMPARATIVES TO EXPRESS CHANGE

*Look at the chart. It shows some food trends (increases and decreases). Complete the statements about the trends. Use the comparative forms of the adjectives in the box to show an increase/decrease or a cause and effect. Use both **more** and **less**.*

| big | cheap | ~~expensive~~ | good | healthy | heavy | popular | varied |

	1985	1995	2005
1. cost of a slice of pizza	$	$$	$$$
2. cost of a microwave oven	$$$	$$	$
3. quality of frozen pizza	+	++	+++
4. restaurant portion size	+	++	+++
5. choice of pizza toppings	+	++	+++
6. popularity of fast food	+	++	+++
7. health quality of fast food	+++	++	+
8. weight of fast-food customers	+	++	+++

1. A slice of pizza is getting _____ *more and more expensive* _____.

2. A microwave oven is getting _____.

3. The quality of frozen pizza is getting _____.

4. The size of portions in restaurants is getting _____.

5. The choice of pizza toppings is getting _____.

6. Fast food is becoming _____.

7. It's also becoming _____.

8. Fast-food customers are becoming _____.

6 | CAUSE AND EFFECT WITH TWO COMPARATIVES

Read the information. Write a similar sentence using two comparatives.

1. When the pizza is salty, I get thirsty.

   The saltier the pizza, the thirstier I get.

(continued)

2. When the ingredients are fresh, the food is good.

_____

3. When the restaurant is popular, the lines are long.

_____

4. When the meal is enjoyable, the customers are satisfied.

_____

5. When the selection is big, the customers are happy.

_____

6. When it's late in the day, the servers get tired.

_____

7. When the restaurant is crowded, the service is slow.

_____

8. When the service is good, the tip is high.

_____

7 | PERSONALIZATION

Write about some trends in your country or city.

1. _____

2. _____

3. _____

4. _____

5. _____

Adjectives: Superlatives

1 | SPELLING: REGULAR AND IRREGULAR SUPERLATIVES

Write the superlative form of the adjectives.

Adjective	Superlative
1. amazing	the most amazing
2. bad	
3. big	
4. cute	
5. dangerous	
6. expensive	
7. far	
8. funny	
9. good	
10. happy	
11. hot	
12. important	
13. intelligent	
14. interesting	
15. low	
16. nice	
17. noisy	
18. practical	
19. warm	
20. wonderful	

2 | THE SUPERLATIVE

Look at the information comparing the subway systems in three cities. Complete the sentences with the superlative form of the adjectives in parentheses. Also, write the name of the correct city.

THREE NORTH AMERICAN SUBWAY SYSTEMS			
	Toronto	**New York City**	**Mexico City**
First opened	1954	1904	1969
Length (km)	64.9	371	202
Number of riders (per year)	410 million	1.3 billion	1.4 billion
Cost of a single ride*	$2.50	$2.00	$0.20

*in U.S. dollars

1. _____*New York City*_____ has _____*the oldest*_____ subway system.
   (old)

2. _____ has _____ subway system.
   (new)

3. _____'s system is _____.
   (long)

4. _____'s system is _____.
   (short)

5. _____ system is in _____.
   (busy)

6. _____ has _____ number of riders.
   (low)

7. The subway in _____ is _____ to use.
   (expensive)

8. You can buy _____ single ticket in _____.
   (cheap)

3 | SUPERLATIVE ADJECTIVES

Read the comments posted on an online subway message board. Complete the sentences with the superlative form of the correct adjectives from the boxes. Use **the -est** *or* **the most / the least**.

Track Talk

beautiful	big	comfortable	easy	new	~~old~~

I just got back from London. Completed in 1863, the tube (that's what they call their

subway) is _____ *the oldest* _____ in the world, but it works just fine!
1.

* * * * * * * * * *

The seats in the New York subway are _____ I've ever
2.

experienced! They are so hard! I heard they used to be made of straw. What happened?

* * * * * * * * * *

Completed just a few years ago, Sheppard Subway is _____
3.

metro line in Toronto. I just rode it. Very nice!

* * * * * * * * * *

IMHO (In my humble opinion), the Moscow subway stations are without question

_____ in the world. With statues, chandeliers, and artwork on
4.

the walls, they look more like museums than stations! Wonderful! It's also one of

_____ systems to use. There are plenty of maps and signs so you
5.

don't get lost. As you can see, I'm one of _____ fans of this great
6.

system!

convenient	cool	dangerous	fast	hot	interesting

I just got back from a week's vacation in New York City. We had a great time, and

rode the subway a lot. It's _____ way to get around town—no
7.

traffic to slow you down. It's summer, and all the trains are air-conditioned. Get ready for

(continued)

one of _____ rides you've ever been on. In contrast, the stations
                          8.

are among _____ I've ever been in. I'm sure the temperature was
                          9.

over 100 degrees. That said, New York has one of _____ systems
                                                            10.

in the world. It's open 24 hours a day, 7 days a week, and you can go all over the place—

even to the beach! And I think it's _____ form of transportation
                                              11.

to take. You see all kinds of people. Really fascinating. And this may really surprise you,

but some people say it's one of _____ subway systems because
                                        12.

there are so many people on it. You're almost never alone—even late at night. I guess

there's safety in numbers!

| crowded | dangerous | efficient | expensive | historic | quiet |

The subway in Athens is probably _____ in the world. When
                                            13.

they were building the system, they found the remains of ancient roads, shops, and baths.

They've made these part of the system.

* * * * * * * * * *

Tokyo has _____ subway in the world. At rush hour there
                    14.

are so many people, special workers help push them onto the trains!

* * * * * * * * * *

Driving in Paris? Don't even think about it! _____ way of
                                                        15.

getting around is the Metro. As in all big cities, you need to be careful and watch your

stuff. Rush hour is definitely _____ time to ride the subway
                                      16.

because there can be pickpockets "working" the trains.

* * * * * * * * * *

I love the subway system in Mexico City. First of all, at just 2 pesos (about 20 cents),

it's _____ ride in town (actually, in the whole world!). And
          17.

because the train has rubber wheels, it's one of _____ rides too.
                                                            18.

4 | EDITING

Read this tourist's postcard. There are seven mistakes in the use of the superlative. The first mistake is already corrected. Find and correct six more.

Hola!

Greetings from Mexico City! With its mixture of the old and the new, this is one of the

most interesting

~~interestingest~~ cities I've ever visited. The people are among the friendlier in the world, and

they have been very patient with my attempts to speak their language. Spanish is definitely

one of a most beautiful languages, and I definitely want to take lessons when I get home.

This has been the most hot summer in years, and I'm looking forward to going to the beach

next week. The air pollution is also the baddest I've experienced, so I'll be glad to be out of

the city. By the way, we definitely did not need to rent a car. The most fast and convenientest

way to get around is by subway.

See you soon.

L.

5 | PERSONALIZATION

Complete these statements about your own life experiences. Use the superlative.

1. _____ in my class.

2. _____ in my school.

3. _____ in my family.

4. _____ in my city.

5. _____ in my country.

6. _____ in the world.

26 Adverbs: *As . . . as,* Comparatives, Superlatives

1 | SPELLING: REGULAR AND IRREGULAR COMPARATIVE AND SUPERLATIVE FORMS OF ADVERBS

Write the comparative and superlative forms of the adverbs.

Adverb	Comparative	Superlative
1. badly	*worse*	*the worst*
2. beautifully		
3. carefully		
4. dangerously		
5. early		
6. far		
7. fast		
8. quickly		
9. soon		
10. well		

2 | COMPARISON OF ADVERBS WITH *AS . . . AS*

Look at these track-and-field records for five athletes. Complete the statements with the words in parentheses and **(not) as . . . as**.

	100-METER RUN	HIGH JUMP	DISCUS THROW
Athlete A	12.0 sec.	1.8 m	37 m
Athlete B	14.0 sec.	1.6 m	39 m
Athlete C	13.5 sec.	1.9 m	38 m
Athlete D	14.0 sec.	1.9 m	39 m
Athlete E	15.0 sec.	2.0 m	40 m

1. Athlete B _____ *didn't run as fast as* _____ Athlete A.
      (run / fast)

2. Athlete B _____ Athlete D.
      (run / fast)

3. Athlete C _____ Athlete D.
      (jump / high)

4. Athlete A _____ Athlete E.
      (jump / high)

5. Athlete C _____ Athlete E.
      (throw the discus / far)

6. Athlete D _____ Athlete B.
      (throw the discus / far)

7. Overall, Athlete B _____ Athlete D.
      (do / good)

8. Overall, Athlete A _____ Athlete C.
      (compete / successful)

3 | THE COMPARATIVE FORM OF ADVERBS

*Basketball players from two teams were talking about their last game. Complete their comments. Use the correct form of the words in parentheses. Use **than** when necessary.*

GEORGE: The other team played well, but we played much _____ *better* _____.
                                                              1. (good)

That's why we won.

⊕ ⊕ ⊕ ⊕

BOB: We played _____ our opponents. We really deserved to win,
                  2. (hard)

and we did.

⊕ ⊕ ⊕ ⊕

ALEX: It wasn't a great game for me. I moved _____ usual because of
                                                3. (slow)

my bad ankle. In a few weeks, I should be able to run _____.
                                                        4. (fast)

I hope that'll help the team.

⊕ ⊕ ⊕ ⊕

RICK: Our shooting was off today. We missed too many baskets. We need to shoot

_____ if we want to win.
5. (accurate)

⊕ ⊕ ⊕ ⊕

(continued)

LARRY: I was surprised by how well they played. They played _____
_____ 6. (aggressive)

they've played in a long time. We couldn't beat them.

⊕ ⊕ ⊕ ⊕

ELVIN: I'm disappointed. We've been playing a lot _____ our
7. (bad)

opponents this season. We have to try to concentrate _____
8. (good)

in order to break this losing streak.

⊕ ⊕ ⊕ ⊕

RANDY: Team spirit was very strong. We played a lot _____ together,
9. (successful)

and it paid off.

⊕ ⊕ ⊕ ⊕

DENNIS: Of course I'm happy with the results. But if we want to keep it up, we have to practice

_____ and _____. I think we just got
10. (serious)   11. (regular)

lucky today.

Now write the names of the players under the correct team.

Winning Team	**Losing Team**
_____George_____	_____
_____	_____
_____	_____
_____	_____

4 | THE COMPARATIVE AND THE SUPERLATIVE OF ADVERBS

*Look at the chart in Exercise 2. Complete the statements with the correct form of the words in parentheses. Use **than** when necessary. Fill in the blanks with the letter of the correct athlete—**A, B, C, D,** or **E.***

1. Athlete B ran _____*faster than*_____ Athlete __E__, but Athlete __A__ ran
   (fast)

   _____*the fastest*_____ of all.
   (fast)

2. Athlete ____ ran _____. He ran _____ all
   (slow)   (slow)

   the other competitors.

3. Athlete A jumped _____ Athlete _____.
   (high)

4. Athlete _____ jumped _____ of all five athletes.
   (high)

5. Athletes B and D didn't throw the discus _____ Athlete _____.
   (far)

6. Athlete _____ threw the discus _____.
   (far)

7. Athlete _____ won in two categories. He performed _____.
   (good)

8. At 15 seconds, Athlete _____ scored _____ in the run, but he did
   (bad)

   _____ the other athletes in the rest of the events.
   (good)

5 | THE COMPARATIVE OF ADVERBS TO EXPRESS CHANGE

Read about some athletes. Write a summary statement about each situation. Use the correct form of the words in the box.

accurate	bad	dangerous	far	~~fast~~
frequent	graceful	hard	high	slow

1. Last month Lisa ran a mile in 12 minutes. This month she's running a mile in 8 minutes.

   SUMMARY: *She's running faster and faster.* _____

2. Last month she ran three times a week. This month she's running every day.

   SUMMARY: _____

3. Last month Josh threw the ball 10 yards. This month he's throwing it 13 yards.

   SUMMARY: _____

4. Last month when Jennifer shot baskets, she got only five balls in. Now when she shoots baskets, she gets at least eight balls in.

   SUMMARY: _____

5. Six months ago, Mike jumped four and a half feet. Now he's jumping almost six feet.

   SUMMARY: _____

6. Matt used to run an 8-minute mile. These days he runs a 10-minute mile.

   SUMMARY: _____

7. The ice-skating team of Sonia and Boris used to get four points for artistic impression. These days they are scoring more than five points.

   SUMMARY: _____

(continued)

8. The basketball team used to practice two hours a day. Now they practice three.

SUMMARY: _____

9. Jason drives a race car. Last year he had two accidents. This year he's had five.

SUMMARY: _____

10. Last year the team felt good about their game. Now they feel terrible.

SUMMARY: _____

6 | EDITING

Read Luisa's exercise journal. There are seven mistakes in the use of adverbs. The first mistake is already corrected. Find and correct six more.

Tuesday, June 11

    I just completed my run. I'm running much longer ~~that~~ *than* before.

Wednesday, June 12

    Today I ran for 30 minutes without getting out of breath. I'm glad I decided to run more slow. The more slowly I run, the farthest I can go. I'm really seeing progress.

Thursday, June 13

    Because I'm enjoying it, I run more and more frequent. And the more often I do it, the longer and farther I can go. I really believe that running helps me feel better more quick than other forms of exercise. I'm even sleeping better than before!

Friday, June 14

    I'm thinking about running in the next marathon. I may not run as fast than younger runners, but I think I can run long and farther. We'll see!

Gerunds: Subject and Object

1 | GERUNDS AS SUBJECT AND AS OBJECT

Complete this article from a health magazine. Use the gerund form of the verbs in parentheses.

KICK UP YOUR HEELS!

In recent years, _____dancing_____ has become a very popular
       1. (dance)

way to stay in shape. In addition to its health benefits, it also has

social advantages. "I really enjoy _____ out and
          2. (go)

_____ new people," says Diana Romero, a 28-year-old word processor.
3. (meet)

"_____ all day at a computer isn't healthy. After work I need to move."
  4. (Sit)

And Diana isn't alone on the dance floor. Many people who dislike _____,
          5. (run)

_____ weights, or _____ sit-ups are swaying to the beat of
  6. (lift)   **7. (do)**

the swing, salsa, and rumba.

   So, if you are looking for an enjoyable way to build muscles and friendships, consider

_____ a spin on one of the many studio dance floors that are opening up in
  8. (take)

cities across the country. "_____ can be fun," says Sandra Carrone, owner
        9. (Exercise)

of Studio Two-Step. So, quit _____ time, grab a partner, and kick up your
        10. (waste)

heels!

2 | GERUNDS AS SUBJECT AND AS OBJECT

Look at the results of this questionnaire on four students' likes and dislikes. Then complete the sentences below with appropriate gerunds.

Key:	+ enjoy
	✓ don't mind
	− dislike

	KATIE	RYAN	LUKE	ANA
Dance	+	+	+	+
Walk	+	+	✓	✓
Do sit-ups	−	−	−	−
Play tennis	+	−	+	✓
Run	−	+	+	+
Lift weights	−	✓	−	+
Swim	✓	+	−	✓
Ride a bike	+	+	✓	+

1. Ryan is the only one who dislikes _____*playing tennis*_____.

2. _____ is the group's favorite activity.

3. Half the people dislike _____.

4. Half the people enjoy _____ and _____.

5. Katie and Ana don't mind _____.

6. Ana is the only one who enjoys _____.

7. Luke doesn't mind _____ or _____.

8. _____ is the most disliked activity.

9. Luke is the only one who dislikes _____.

10. He also doesn't like _____ or _____.

11. Katie is the only one who doesn't like _____.

12. Katie and Luke really like _____, but Ryan dislikes it.

13. _____ is the group's second favorite activity.

14. Ryan doesn't mind _____.

3 | GERUNDS AFTER CERTAIN VERBS

Sandra Carrone is having a dance party at her studio. Complete the summary sentences with the appropriate verbs from the box and the gerund form of the verbs in parentheses.

admit	consider	deny	dislike	enjoy
keep	mind	~~quit~~	regret	suggest

1. LUKE: Would you like a cup of coffee?

    KATIE: No, thanks. I haven't had coffee in five years.

    SUMMARY: Katie _____*quit drinking*_____ coffee five years ago.
    (drink)

2. OSCAR: Oh, they're playing a tango. Would you like to dance?

    RIKA: No, thanks. It's not my favorite dance.

    SUMMARY: Rika _____ the tango.
    (do)

3. ANA: Do you often come to these dance parties?

    MARIA: Yes. It's a good opportunity to dance with a lot of different partners.

    SUMMARY: Maria _____ with different partners.
    (dance)

4. LAURA: I don't know how to do the cha-cha. Could you show me?

    BILL: OK. Just follow me.

    SUMMARY: Bill doesn't _____ Laura the cha-cha.
    (teach)

5. KATIE: This is a difficult dance. How did you learn it?

    LUKE: I practiced it over and over again.

    SUMMARY: Luke _____ the dance.
    (practice)

6. VERA: Ow. You stepped on my toe!

    LUIS: No, I didn't!

    SUMMARY: Luis _____ on Vera's toe.
    (step)

7. BILL: Are you going to take any more classes?

    LAURA: I'm not sure. I haven't decided yet. Maybe.

    SUMMARY: Laura is _____ more dance classes.
    (take)

(continued)

8.　　**KATIE:** I really love dancing.

　　　LUKE: Me too. I'm sorry I didn't start years ago. It's a lot of fun.

　SUMMARY: Luke _____ dance lessons sooner.
　　　　　　　　　　　　(not begin)

9.　　**BILL:** Why don't we go out for coffee after class next week?

　　　LAURA: OK. I'd like that.

　SUMMARY: Bill _____ out after class.
　　　　　　　　　　　　(go)

10.　　**LUKE:** You look tired.

　　　LAURA: I *am* tired. I think this will be the last dance for me.

　SUMMARY: Laura _____ tired.
　　　　　　　　　　　　(feel)

4 | PERSONALIZATION

Look at the chart in Exercise 2. How do you feel about the eight activities in the chart?
*Write sentences using **enjoy**, **don't mind**, or **dislike**. If you have never done an activity,*
begin your sentence with: **I (don't) think I would enjoy . . .**

1. _____

2. _____

3. _____

4. _____

5. _____

6. _____

7. _____

8. _____

Now write about some other activities.

9. _____

10. _____

Gerunds After Prepositions

1 | PREPOSITIONS AFTER CERTAIN VERBS AND ADJECTIVES

Complete the chart with the prepositions from the box. You will use some prepositions more than once.

about	for	in	of	on	to

1. apologize _____*for*_____

2. approve _____

3. be opposed _____

4. be tired _____

5. be used _____

6. be worried _____

7. believe _____

8. insist _____

9. look forward _____

10. succeed _____

2 | GERUNDS AFTER PREPOSITIONS

These conversations took place at a student council meeting. Complete the summary sentence for each conversation. Use an expression from Exercise 1 and the gerund form of the verbs in parentheses.

1.   **KYLE:** Where were you? It's 7:30. Our meeting started at 7:00.

    JOHN: I know. I'm sorry.

    SUMMARY: John _____*apologized for coming*_____ late.
                             (come)

(continued)

2.   MATT: I have some good news. We've reached our goal. Since our last meeting, we've

        collected more than 100 student signatures in favor of going on strike.

SUMMARY: The students _____ more than 100 signatures.
                              (collect)

3.   ANA: I'm not so sure it's a good idea to strike.

    JOHN: Final exams are in a few weeks. It'll be a problem if we miss classes.

SUMMARY: John _____ classes.
                     (miss)

4.   ANA: I don't know. We've always solved our problems with the administration before.

    JOHN: That's true. In the past, they've always listened to us.

SUMMARY: These students _____ together with the
                                 (work)

    administration.

5.   ANA: I'm against striking. We should talk to the administration again.

    JOHN: I agree. That's the best way to solve this problem.

SUMMARY: Ana and John _____ to the administration again.
                             (talk)

6.   MATT: We keep asking the administration for a response. They've said nothing.

    EVA: That's right. We've had enough. We don't want to wait anymore.

SUMMARY: These students _____ for an answer.
                             (wait)

7.   JOHN: Can we give this decision a little more time?

    MATT: No, I'm sorry. We really *have to* reach a decision today.

SUMMARY: Matt _____ a decision immediately.
                     (reach)

8.   MATT: Let's take a vote. All those in favor of going on strike, raise your hand. . . . OK.

    That's ten for and two against. We'll recommend a strike to the student body.

SUMMARY: The Student Council _____ a strike.
                             (have)

9.   EVA: Only two people voted no.

SUMMARY: Only two council members _____ on strike.
                                 (go)

10.   ANA: I don't know about you, but I'll be glad when all this is over.

    JOHN: I know what you mean. I'll be happy when things return to normal.

SUMMARY: Ana and John are _____ to their normal activities.
                           (return)

3 | GERUNDS AFTER PREPOSITIONS

Read this editorial from a student newspaper. Complete the article with the gerund form of the verbs from the box.

be	fire	get	~~go~~	listen	make
miss	permit	see	strike	try	

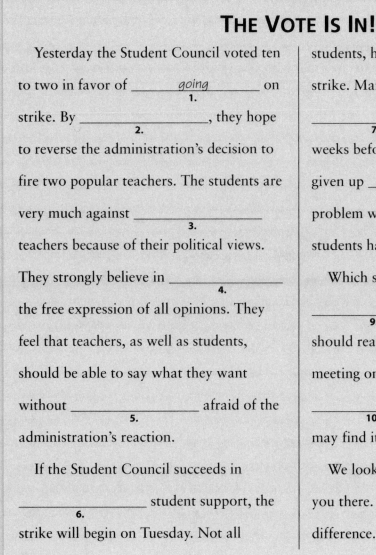

THE VOTE IS IN!

Yesterday the Student Council voted ten to two in favor of _____going_____ on **1.** strike. By _____, they hope **2.** to reverse the administration's decision to fire two popular teachers. The students are very much against _____ **3.** teachers because of their political views. They strongly believe in _____ **4.** the free expression of all opinions. They feel that teachers, as well as students, should be able to say what they want without _____ afraid of the **5.** administration's reaction.

If the Student Council succeeds in _____ student support, the **6.** strike will begin on Tuesday. Not all students, however, support the idea of a strike. Many students are very afraid of _____ classes just a few **7.** weeks before exam time. They haven't given up _____ to solve the **8.** problem with the administration. Other students haven't made up their minds yet.

Which side are you on? Before _____ a final decision, you **9.** should really attend the next Council meeting on Monday at 4:00. Then after _____ to both sides, you **10.** may find it easier to make a decision.

We look forward to _____ **11.** you there. Together we can make a big difference.

4 | PERSONALIZATION

How do you feel about school? Complete these sentences by adding a preposition and a gerund.

1. I'm looking forward _____

2. I'm a little worried _____

3. I've gotten used _____

4. I sometimes get tired _____

5. I'm excited _____

6. I'm in favor _____

7. I'm opposed _____

Infinitives
After Certain Verbs

1 | INFINITIVES AFTER CERTAIN VERBS

Read this exchange of letters in an advice column. Complete the letters with the correct form of the verbs in parentheses. Use the simple present, simple past, or future for the first verb.

Dear Annie,

I've known John for two years. Last month, after a lot of

discussion, we _____decided to get_____ married next
          1. (decide / get)

summer. Since then, our relationship has been a nightmare. John

criticizes me for every little thing, and we are constantly fighting. I

_____ a marriage counselor, but John
    2. (want / see)

_____ with me. Then, last night, he even
    3. (refuse / go)

_____ the relationship if I mention the idea of counseling again.
4. (threaten / end)

I don't understand what's going on. We used to get along great. I still love John, but I

_____ the next step. What should I do?
5. (hesitate / take)

ONE FOOT OUT THE DOOR

Dear One Foot Out the Door,

I've heard your story many times before. You're right to be concerned. John

_____ afraid of getting married. As soon as you got engaged, he
    6. (seem / be)

_____ distance by fighting with you. I agree that counseling is a
    7. (attempt / create)

good idea if the two of you really _____ together. Maybe each of
             8. (intend / stay)

you _____ to a counselor separately before going to one together.
  9. (need / speak)

It's possible that John _____ alone to discuss some of his fears.
       10. (agree / go)

ANNIE

2 | VERB + INFINITIVE OR VERB + OBJECT + INFINITIVE

Read some conversations between men and women in relationships. Complete the two summary statements for each conversation.

1. **SHE:** I *really* think you should see a therapist.

   HE: I'm not going to.

   SUMMARY: She urged _him to see a therapist._____

   He refused _to see a therapist._____

2. **HE:** Could you please do the dishes tonight?

   SHE: Sorry. I don't have time. Could you please do them?

   SUMMARY: He didn't want _____

   She wanted _____

3. **HE:** Don't forget to buy some milk.

   SHE: OK. I'll get some on the way home.

   SUMMARY: He reminded_____

   She agreed _____

4. **SHE:** Will you do me a favor? Could you drive me to my aunt's?

   HE: OK.

   SUMMARY: She asked _____

   He agreed _____

5. **SHE:** Would you like to have dinner at my place Friday night?

   HE: Um . . . I'm not sure. Um . . . I guess so.

   SUMMARY: She invited _____

   He hesitated _____

6. **SHE:** Will you give me your answer tomorrow?

   HE: Yes, I will. That's a promise.

   SUMMARY: She wants _____

   He promised _____

7. **SHE:** Would you like me to cut your hair? It's really long.

   HE: Oh, OK.

   SUMMARY: She offered _____

   He is going to allow _____

8.   **SHE:** It's 8:00. I thought you said you'd be home at 7:00.

      HE: No. I always get home at 8:00.

  SUMMARY: She expected _____

            He expected _____

9.   **HE:** Could you call me before you leave the office?

    SHE: I was going to, but I forgot.

  SUMMARY: He would like _____

            She intended _____

10.   **SHE:** Let's see a movie Friday night.

     HE: OK, but could you pick one out?

  SUMMARY: She would like _____

            He would like _____

3 | EDITING

Read this journal entry. There are nine mistakes in the use of infinitives. The first mistake is already corrected. Find and correct eight more.

Friday, October 15

Annie answered my letter! She advised ~~we~~ *us* to go to counseling separately. I don't know if John will agree going, but I'm going to ask him to think about it. I attempted to introduce the topic last night, but he pretended to not hear me. I won't give up, though. I'm going to try to persuade he to go. If he agrees to go, I may ask Annie recommend some counselors in our area. I want finding someone really good. Our relationship deserves to have a chance, and I'm prepared give it one. But I want John feels the same way. I need to know that he's 100% committed to the relationship. I can be patient, but I can't afford waiting forever.

4 | PERSONALIZATION

What do you expect from your friends? Write about yourself. Use infinitives.

1. I expect _____

2. I would like _____

3. I urge _____

4. I try to persuade _____

5. _____

6. _____

Infinitives of Purpose

1 | AFFIRMATIVE AND NEGATIVE STATEMENTS

Combine these pairs of sentences. Use the infinitive of purpose.

1. Ned got a job at Edge Electronics. He needs to earn money for school.

   Ned got a job at Edge Electronics to earn money for school.

2. Ned never brings money to work. He doesn't want to buy a lot of stuff.

   Ned never brings money to work in order not to buy a lot of stuff.

3. He uses most of his salary. He has to pay his college tuition.

   _____

4. He really wants an MP3 player. He wants to download music from the Internet.

   _____

5. He's going to wait for a sale. Then he won't pay the full price.

   _____

6. A lot of people came into the store today. They looked at the new gadgets.

   _____

7. They like talking to Ned. They want to get information about the gadgets.

   _____

8. Someone bought an electronic navigator. He doesn't want to get lost.

   _____

9. Another person bought a tiny camcorder. She wants to bring it on vacation.

   _____

(continued)

10. She used her credit card. She didn't want to pay right away.

_____

11. Ned showed her how to use the camcorder. Now she can do a lot of things.

_____

12. She'll use it as a camera. She'll take videos.

_____

2 | AFFIRMATIVE AND NEGATIVE STATEMENTS

Some people are talking at a mall. Complete the conversations with the verbs in the box and the infinitive of purpose.

carry	cut	~~find~~	find out	have
miss	pay	return	sign	waste

1. **A:** I need to look at the mall directory.

   B: How come?

   A: _____ *To find* _____ Edge Electronics. I hear they've opened a new store here.

2. **A:** I'd like to return this.

   B: Do you have the receipt?

   A: No, I don't. I got it as a gift, and I really can't use it.

   B: Hmmm. I see there's no price tag on it. I'm sorry, but you need the receipt or the price tag

   _____ it.

3. **A:** Do you always pay by credit card?

   B: No. I don't like to pay finance charges. It ends up being more expensive that way.

   A: I know. I always pay the bill immediately _____ a finance charge.

4. **A:** Can I please have a shopping bag?

   B: Sure.

   A: Thanks. I need one _____ all this stuff.

5. **A:** Do you have a pen?

   B: Here you are.

   A: Thanks. I need one _____ my name.

6. **A:** I'm hungry.

   B: Me too. Let's go to the food court _____ a snack.

   A: Good idea. I always get hungry when I'm shopping.

7. **A:** Do you have a sharper knife? I need one _____ this steak. It's a

   little tough.

   B: I'm sorry. I'll bring you one right away.

8. **A:** How do those shoes fit?

   B: I'm not sure. They may be a little tight.

   A: Walk around a little _____ if they're the right size.

9. **A:** We should leave now.

   B: Why? It's only 5:00.

   A: I know. But we have to leave right now _____ the express bus.

10. **A:** Here's the up escalator, but where's the escalator going down?

    B: Oh, let's just take the elevator _____ time.

3 | EDITING

Read this note. There are five mistakes in the use of the infinitive of purpose. The first mistake is already corrected. Find and correct four more.

Eva—

I went to the store ~~for~~ ^{to} get some eggs and other things for dinner. I set the

alarm on the electronic organizer to remind you to put the turkey in the oven.

Could you call Cindi too ask her to bring some dessert? Tell her she should come

straight from school in order to be not late. We'll eat at 6:00—if that's OK

with you. Remember—you can use the organizer for checking the vegetable

casserole recipe. I've got to run in order to get back in time to help you!

Could I use your new camcorder order to film the event?

M.

1 | WORD ORDER

Unscramble the words to write statements about a student newspaper.

1. is / this voting-rights story / enough / to put on the front page / interesting

   <u>This voting-rights story is interesting enough to put on the front page.</u> +

2. to fit on one page / long / the story / too / is

   _____

3. enough / to give us an interview / Ed Smith / nice / was

   _____

4. for us / to use / these computers / too / are getting / old

   _____

5. aren't / low / the bookshelves / to reach / for me / enough

   _____

6. to win an award / enough / has gotten / this newspaper / good

   _____

7. too / it's / noisy / for me / to concentrate

   _____

8. busy / are / the students / to take a break / too

   _____

9. to work on a major newspaper / good / is / Tina / enough

   _____

Now look at the sentences you wrote. Put a plus sign (+) next to all the positive points. Put a minus sign (−) next to all the negative points.

2 | INFINITIVES WITH *TOO* AND *ENOUGH*

Some people are talking at the office of a student newspaper. Complete the conversations.
Use the words in parentheses with the infinitive and **too** *or* **enough**.

1. **A:** Can you read Tina's handwriting?

   B: No. It's _____*too messy for me to read*_____.
   (messy / me / read)

2. **A:** It's noon. Do you think we can call Ed Smith in San Francisco?

   B: Sure. It's 9:00 A.M. there. That's _____.
   (late / call)

3. **A:** Could you help me with those boxes?

   B: Sorry. They're _____. I got hurt at football practice
   (heavy / me / lift)
   yesterday.

4. **A:** You're not drinking your coffee! What's the matter with it?

   B: It's _____. It tastes like someone put about four
   (sweet / drink)
   tablespoons of sugar in it.

5. **A:** Do you think we can put the fax machine on that shelf?

   B: Sure. It's _____.
   (small / fit)

6. **A:** Can you keep the noise down, please? It's _____.
   (noisy / me / think)

   B: Sorry. We'll try to be quieter.

7. **A:** Did you hear that Kyle is graduating?

   B: You're kidding! He's not even 17. He's _____.
   (young / graduate)

8. **A:** Can you turn on the air conditioner, please?

   B: The air conditioner? It's _____ the air conditioner.
   (hot / need)
   What are you going to do in August when it really gets hot?

9. **A:** You sound really sick. Maybe you should call the doctor.

   B: Oh, I'm _____ the doctor. I just need to get some rest.
   (sick / call)

10. **A:** Can you help me get that book? It's _____.
    (high / me / reach)

    B: Sure.

11. **A:** Are you working late today?

    B: No. I'm _____ late today.
    (tired / stay)

12. **A:** What do you think of Tina's article?

    B: It's great. I think it's _____ on the first page.
    (good / go)

3 | EDITING

*Read these posts to an online bulletin board for teens. There are nine mistakes in the use of infinitives with **too** and **enough**. The first mistake is already corrected. Find and correct eight more.*

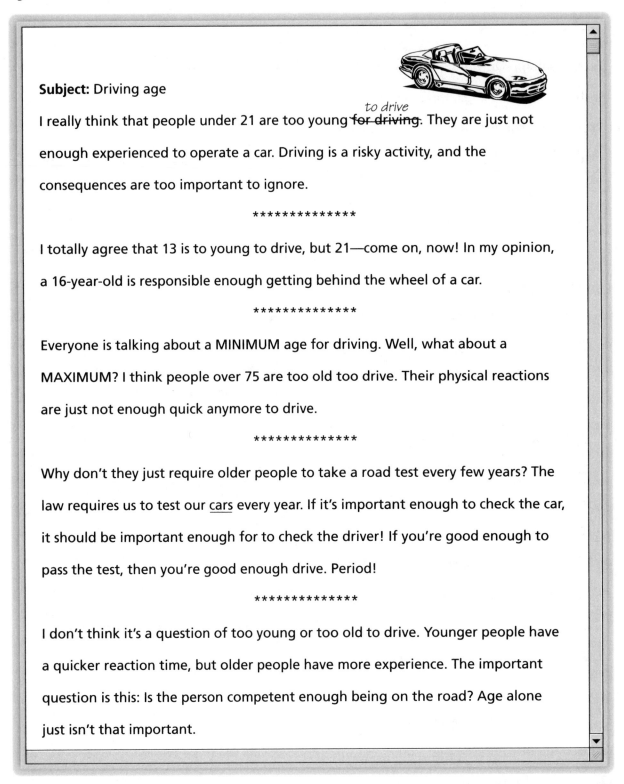

Subject: Driving age

I really think that people under 21 are too young ~~for driving~~. *to drive* They are just not

enough experienced to operate a car. Driving is a risky activity, and the

consequences are too important to ignore.

****

I totally agree that 13 is to young to drive, but 21—come on, now! In my opinion,

a 16-year-old is responsible enough getting behind the wheel of a car.

****

Everyone is talking about a MINIMUM age for driving. Well, what about a

MAXIMUM? I think people over 75 are too old too drive. Their physical reactions

are just not enough quick anymore to drive.

****

Why don't they just require older people to take a road test every few years? The

law requires us to test our cars every year. If it's important enough to check the car,

it should be important enough for to check the driver! If you're good enough to

pass the test, then you're good enough drive. Period!

****

I don't think it's a question of too young or too old to drive. Younger people have

a quicker reaction time, but older people have more experience. The important

question is this: Is the person competent enough being on the road? Age alone

just isn't that important.

4 | PERSONALIZATION

*Write your own opinions about the driving age. Use **too** and **enough** with the infinitive.*

_____

_____

_____

_____

_____

_____

_____

_____

_____

_____

_____

UNIT 32 | Gerunds and Infinitives

1 | GERUND OR INFINITIVE

Read this notice about a support-group meeting for people who are afraid of flying. Complete the sentences with the correct form—gerund or infinitive—of the verbs in parentheses.

Stuck on the ground? Get help!

Are you afraid of _____*flying*_____? Stop _____ in fear!
                1. (fly)   **2. (live)**

_____ is the safest form of transportation, but many people are too afraid
3. (Fly)

_____ on a plane.
4. (get)

Do *you* avoid _____ because you're afraid to leave the ground? Would you
                    5. (fly)

like _____ your fear?
    6. (get over)

Don't let your fear prevent you from _____ all the things that you want
                               7. (do)

_____. You deserve _____ a life free of fear.
8. (do)   **9. (live)**

Decide _____ something about your problem now. Come to our monthly
          10. (do)

support-group meetings.

The next meeting is at 7:00 P.M., Tuesday, March 3 at the Community Center. We look

forward to _____ you there.
       11. (see)

And don't forget _____ our website at www.flyaway.com for some helpful
             12. (visit)

tips on _____ yourself off the ground!
     13. (get)

2 | GERUND OR INFINITIVE

These conversations took place at a support-group meeting for people afraid of flying. Complete the summary statements about the people. Use the correct verbs or expressions from the box and the gerund or infinitive form of the verbs in parentheses.

afford	agree	be tired of	believe in	~~enjoy~~	forget
intend	offer	quit	refuse	remember	stop

1. JASON: Have you ever been to one of these support-group meetings before?

    AMBER: Yes. I like meeting people with the same problem. You get a lot of useful tips.

    SUMMARY: Amber _____*enjoys meeting*_____ people with the same problem.

(meet)

2. ANDREA: Why did you start coming to these meetings?

    HANK: My fear of flying prevents me from doing too many things. I finally want to do

    something about it.

    SUMMARY: Hank _____ afraid of flying.

(be)

3. DYLAN: Would you like a cup of coffee?

    SYLVIE: No, thanks. I gave up coffee. It makes me too nervous.

    SUMMARY: Sylvie _____ coffee.

(drink)

4. CARYN: I think these meetings are really helpful. You can learn a lot when you talk to other

    people about your problems.

    PAULO: I agree.

    SUMMARY: Caryn _____ to other people about her problems.

(talk)

5. MARY: Did you bring the travel guide?

    SARA: Oh, no. I left it at work.

    SUMMARY: Sara _____ the travel guide.

(bring)

6. AMANDA: Did you tell Amy about tonight's meeting?

    JOSHUA: No, *you* told Amy about the meeting. I heard you do it.

    AMANDA: Really? Are you sure?

    SUMMARY: Amanda doesn't _____ Amy about the meeting.

(tell)

(continued)

7. **TYLER:** You're late. I was getting worried.

EMILY: I'm sorry. On the way over here, I noticed that I was almost out of gas.

So I went to fill up the tank.

SUMMARY: Emily _____ gas.
                            (get)

8. **KATIE:** I know your parents live in California. How do you get there?

MIKE: I take the train. It's a long trip, and I lose much too much time.

SUMMARY: Mike can't _____ the time.
                                (lose)

9. **CAMILLE:** I was afraid to come to the meeting tonight.

VILMA: Well, I just *won't* live in fear.

SUMMARY: Vilma _____ in fear.
                              (live)

10. **ERIN:** Have you made your flight reservations yet?

LUIS: Not yet. But I'm definitely going to do it.

SUMMARY: Luis _____ a reservation.
                            (make)

11. **RACHEL:** Do you think you could help us organize the next meeting?

JUSTIN: Sure. When is it scheduled for?

RACHEL: We don't have a date yet, but I'll let you know.

SUMMARY: Justin _____ with the next meeting.
                            (help)

12. **AXEL:** Would you like a ride home?

JOANNA: Thanks. That would be great.

SUMMARY: Axel _____ Joanna home.
                        (drive)

3 | GERUND OR INFINITIVE

Rewrite these sentences. If the sentence uses the gerund, rewrite it with the infinitive. If the sentence uses the infinitive, rewrite it with the gerund.

1. It's important to talk about your problems.

   Talking about your problems is important.

2. Going to a support group is helpful.

   It's helpful to go to a support group.

3. Working together is useful.

   _____

4. It's smart to be careful.

_____

5. It's not good to be afraid all the time.

_____

6. Flying isn't dangerous.

_____

7. Doing relaxation exercises is a good idea.

_____

8. Traveling is wonderful.

_____

4 | PERSONALIZATION

Write about things you do when you feel nervous or afraid. Use gerunds and infinitives.

1. I avoid _____

2. I always try _____

3. It's important _____

4. I keep_____

5. I try to remember _____

6. _____

UNIT

33 Preferences: *Prefer, Would prefer, Would rather*

1 | AFFIRMATIVE STATEMENTS

Alicia ranked the following leisure-time activities according to her preferences.
1 = what she likes most; 10 = what she likes least.

Leisure-Time Preferences

_5_ cook

_3_ watch TV

_2_ go to the movies

_1_ read a book

_10_ play computer games

_9_ surf the net

_4_ hang out with friends

_7_ talk on the phone

_6_ eat out

_8_ listen to music

Complete the sentences about Alicia's preferences.

1. cook / eat out

Alicia prefers *cooking to eating out.* _____

2. listen to music / surf the net

She'd rather _____

3. read a book / hang out with friends

She prefers _____

4. hang out with friends / talk on the phone

She prefers _____

5. watch TV / go to the movies

   She'd rather _____

6. talk on the phone / listen to music

   She'd rather _____

7. play computer games / go to the movies

   She prefers _____

8. watch TV / listen to music

   She prefers _____

9. read a book / watch TV

   She'd rather _____

10. play computer games / read a book

    She prefers _____

2 | AFFIRMATIVE AND NEGATIVE STATEMENTS

Ralph is in the hospital. Look at his completed meal form.

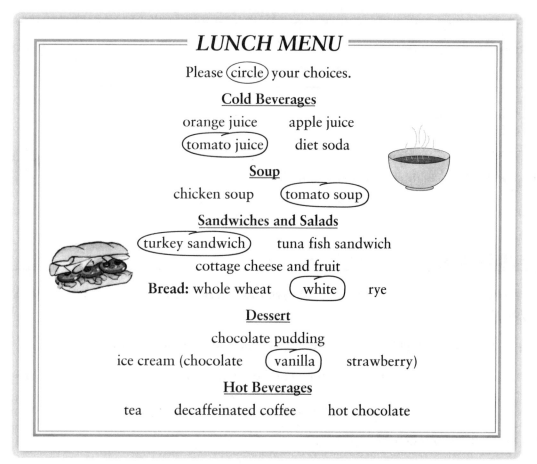

(continued)

Use the cues to write sentences about Ralph's preferences. You may need to change the order of the cues.

1. He'd rather / diet soda

He'd rather not have diet soda.

2. He'd prefer / juice

_____

3. He'd rather / apple juice / tomato juice

_____

4. He'd rather / a hot beverage

_____

5. He'd prefer / chicken soup

_____

6. He'd prefer / a sandwich / cottage cheese and fruit

_____

7. He'd prefer / a tuna fish sandwich / a turkey sandwich

_____

8. He'd rather / white bread

_____

9. He'd rather / chocolate pudding

_____

10. He'd prefer / chocolate ice cream / vanilla ice cream

_____

3 | QUESTIONS

*Complete these conversations with **do you prefer**, **would you prefer**, or **would you rather**.*

1. A: _____ *Do you prefer* _____ watching TV or going to the movies?

B: It really depends. If there's something good on TV, I like doing that.

2. A: _____ newspapers to magazines?

B: Oh, I definitely prefer newspapers.

3. **A:** I don't feel like going out.

   B: _____ to stay home?

   A: Yes, I think I would.

4. **A:** I've got vanilla and chocolate ice cream. Which _____ have?

   B: Chocolate, please.

5. **A:** I thought we could stay home tonight.

   B: Really?

   A: _____ to go out?

   B: Well, there's a good movie at the Quad.

6. **A:** There's a show at 8:00 and one at 10:00. _____ the early or

   the late show?

   B: Let's go to the early show.

7. **A:** Could you get me some juice?

   B: Sure. _____ orange or grapefruit?

   A: Orange, please.

8. **A:** How do you like to spend your free time? _____ doing things

   with friends or doing things alone?

   B: It depends. I need time for my friends, and I need time to be alone.

4 | PERSONALIZATION

Look at the menu in Exercise 2. Complete these sentences with true information.

1. I'd prefer _____

2. I'd prefer not _____

3. I'd rather _____

4. I'd rather not _____

5. I always prefer _____

34 Necessity: *Have (got) to, Must, Don't have to, Must not, Can't*

1 | AFFIRMATIVE AND NEGATIVE STATEMENTS WITH *MUST*

*Read these driving rules. Complete the sentences with **must** or **must not** and the verbs in the box.*

change	drink	drive	forget	~~have~~	know	leave
obey	pass	sit	stop	talk	turn on	wear

1. In almost all countries, you _____*must have*_____ a license in order to drive.

2. You _____ a road test to get a license.

3. You _____ to carry your license with you at all times.

4. You _____ all traffic signs. They are there for a reason!

5. When you see a stop sign, you _____. Don't just slow down.

6. You _____ faster than the maximum speed limit.

7. You _____ lanes without signaling.

8. When it's dark, you _____ your headlights.

9. You _____ the scene of an accident. Wait until the police arrive.

10. In most countries, the driver and passengers _____ seat belts.

11. In some places, you _____ on a cell phone unless you have a headset.

12. Small children _____ in a special safety seat.

13. Alcohol and driving don't mix. You _____ absolutely never

    _____ and drive.

14. Driving laws differ from country to country. You _____ the rules

    before you take to the road in a foreign country!

2 | AFFIRMATIVE AND NEGATIVE STATEMENTS WITH *HAVE TO*

Read about driving rules in different countries. Complete the statements with the correct form of **have to** *or* **don't have to** *and the verbs in parentheses.*

	Minimum driving age	Maximum speed limit on major highway	Side of road	Seat belt law	Warning triangle	First-aid kit	Motorcycle helmet
Australia	16–18*	68 mph/ 110 kmh	left	driver and passengers	no	no	yes
Canada	16	62 mph/ 100 kmh	right	driver and passengers	no	no	yes
Germany	18	none	right	driver and passengers	yes (1)	yes	yes
Italy	18	81 mph/ 130 kmh	right	driver and passengers	yes (1)	recommended	yes
Mexico	18	62 mph/ 100 kmh	right	driver only	no	no	no
Turkey	18	74 mph/ 120 kmh	right	driver and passengers	yes (2)	yes	yes

*depends on the part of the country

1. You _____*have to be*_____ 18 years old to drive in most of the countries.
   (be)

2. You _____ 18 in Canada and some parts of Australia.
   (be)

3. You _____ slower than 81 mph (130 kmh) in Turkey.
   (drive)

4. A driver _____ slower than 81 mph (130 kmh) in Germany.
   (drive)

5. In Australia, drivers _____ on the left side of the road.
   (drive)

6. In Mexico, passengers _____ a seat belt.
   (wear)

7. In Turkey, both the driver and passengers _____ a seat belt.
   (wear)

8. Turkish cars _____ two warning triangles to use in case there is
   (have)
   an accident.

9. In Germany, cars _____ two warning triangles.
   (have)

10. In Germany and Turkey, you _____ a first-aid kit in your car.
    (keep)

11. In Italy, you _____ one in your car.
    (keep)

12. In all of the countries except Mexico, motorcycle riders _____ a helmet.
    (wear)

3 | CONTRAST: *MUST NOT* OR *DON'T HAVE TO*

Look again at the chart in Exercise 2. Complete these statements with **must not** *or the correct form of* **don't have to***.*

1. If you are under the age of 18, you _____ *must not* _____ drive in most of the countries.

2. You _____ be 18 to drive in Canada.

3. You _____ obey a speed limit on major German highways.

4. In Turkey, you _____ drive on the left side of the road.

5. In Mexico, passengers _____ wear seat belts.

6. In Australia, your car _____ have a warning triangle.

7. You _____ drive without a first-aid kit in Germany and Turkey.

8. You _____ have a first-aid kit in Italy.

9. In Mexico, motorcycle riders _____ wear a helmet.

10. In all of the other countries, you _____ ride a motorcycle without wearing a helmet.

4 | STATEMENTS, QUESTIONS, AND SHORT ANSWERS WITH *HAVE TO*

Complete the conversations with short answers or the correct form of **have to** *(present, past, future, or present perfect) and the verbs in parentheses.*

1. **A:** Did you pass your road test the first time you took it?

   B: No. I _____ *had to take* _____ it two more times before I passed!
   $\qquad$ (take)

2. **A:** _____ we _____ for gas?
   $\qquad$ (stop)

   B: _____. The tank's almost empty.

3. **A:** How many times _____ you _____ public
   $\qquad$ (use)

   transportation since you moved here?

   B: Only once. When my car broke down.

4. **A:** _____ you _____ late yesterday?
   $\qquad$ (work)

   B: _____. Luckily, I finished on time.

5. **A:** Are you thinking of buying a new car?

   B: Not yet. But in a couple of years, I _____ another one.
   $\qquad$ (get)

6. **A:** Why didn't you come to the meeting last night?

   B: I _____ my uncle to the airport.

(drive)

7. **A:** My wife got a speeding ticket last week.

   B: Really? How much _____ she _____?

(pay)

   A: It was more than $100.

8. **A:** _____ your son ever _____ for a traffic violation?

(pay)

   B: _____. He's a very careful driver.

9. **A:** _____ you _____ a new license when you move?

(get)

   B: _____. You can only use an out-of-state license for 10 days.

10. **A:** Do you have car insurance?

    B: Of course. Everyone in this country _____ car insurance.

(have)

5 | CONTRAST: *MUST, MUST NOT, HAVE TO, DON'T HAVE TO,* AND *CAN'T*

Read these test questions about road signs in the United States. Write the letter of the correct answer in the box.

1. When you see [YIELD] it means:

   a. You must come to a complete stop.
   b. You must not stop.
   c. You don't have to stop, but you must slow down and prepare to stop if necessary.

   ANS
   C

2. When you see [STOP] it means:

   a. You don't have to stop.
   b. You must stop.
   c. You can't stop.

   ANS

3. When you see [SPEED LIMIT 50] it means:

   a. You must drive 50 miles per hour.
   b. You must not drive faster than 50 miles per hour.
   c. You don't have to drive more than 50 miles per hour.

   ANS

(continued)

4. When you see | NO TURN ON RED | it means:

    a. You have to turn when the light is red.
    b. You don't have to turn when the light is red.
    c. You must not turn when the light is red.

ANS ☐

5. When you see | DO NOT ENTER | it means:

    a. You must not enter.
    b. You don't have to enter.
    c. You must enter.

ANS ☐

6. When you see | DO NOT PASS | it means:

    a. You don't have to pass another car.
    b. You can't pass another car.
    c. You have to pass another car.

ANS ☐

7. When you see | ONE WAY ▶ | it means:

    a. You must drive in the direction of the arrow.
    b. You must not drive in the direction of the arrow.
    c. You don't have to drive in the direction of the arrow.

ANS ☐

8. When you see | MAXIMUM SPEED 65 / MINIMUM SPEED 45 | it means:

    a. You have to drive 45 miles per hour or slower.
    b. You can't drive 70 miles per hour.
    c. You don't have to drive 70 miles per hour.

ANS ☐

6 | PERSONALIZATION

Complete these sentences with information about yourself.

1. Next week, I have to _____

2. I don't have to _____

3. I must not _____

4. I can't _____

5. Last week _____

6. Since last year, _____

Expectations:
Be supposed to

1 | AFFIRMATIVE AND NEGATIVE STATEMENTS WITH *BE SUPPOSED TO*

Today, in some countries, when people get married, the groom's family often shares the expenses, and older couples often pay for their own weddings. However, some people are still traditional. Read the chart and complete the sentences with a form of **be supposed to**.

TRADITIONAL DIVISION OF WEDDING EXPENSES	
Responsibilities of the Bride's Family	**Responsibilities of the Groom's Family**
send invitations pay for food supply flowers pay for the groom's ring provide music	pay for the bride's ring give a rehearsal dinner pay for the honeymoon

1. The groom's parents _____*aren't supposed to send*_____ the invitations.

2. The bride's family _____ the invitations.

3. The bride's parents _____ the music.

4. The groom's parents _____ the music.

5. The groom's family _____ the groom's ring.

6. The groom's family _____ the bride's ring.

7. The bride's parents _____ the honeymoon.

8. The groom's family _____ the honeymoon.

9. The bride's parents _____ the rehearsal dinner.

10. The groom's parents _____ the rehearsal dinner.

11. The groom's family _____ the flowers.

12. The bride's family _____ the food.

2 | AFFIRMATIVE AND NEGATIVE STATEMENTS WITH *BE SUPPOSED TO*

*Erica Nelson is getting married. She completed this change-of-address form, but she made eight mistakes. Find the mistakes and write sentences with **was supposed to** and **wasn't supposed to**. Include the number of the item that has the mistake.*

U.S. Postal Sevice CHANGE OF ADDRESS ORDER	Customer Instructions: Complete Items 1 thru 9, Except Item 8, please PRINT all information including address on face of card.	OFFICIAL USE ONLY

1. Change of address for *(Check one)* ☑ Individual ☑ Entire Family ☐ Business

Zone/Route Id No.

2. Start Date   Month `3 0` Day `0 6` Year `9 5`

3. If TEMPORARY address, print date to discontinue forwarding   Month   Day   Year

Date Entered on Form 3982   M M   D D   Y Y

4. <u>Print</u> Last Name or Name of Business *(If more than one use, use separate Change of Address Order Form for each)*
`E R I C A`

Expiration Date   M M   D D   Y Y

5. <u>Print</u> First Name of Head of Household (include Jr., Sr., etc.). Leave Blank if the Change of Address Order is for a business.
`N e l s o n`

Clerk/Carrier Endorsements

6. <u>Print</u> OLD mailing address, number and street *(if Puerto Rico, include urbanization zone)*
`2 6   M A P L E   R O A D`

Apt./Suite No. `4 A`   P.O. Box No.   R.R/HCR No.   Rural Box/HCR Box No.

City `B O S T O N`   State `M A`   Zip Code `–`

7. <u>Print</u> **NEW** Mailing address, number and street *(if Puerto Rico, include urbanization zone)*
`2 9 8 7   C O S B Y   A V E`

Apt./Suite No.   P.O. Box No.   R.R/HCR No.   Rural Box/HCR Box No.

City `A M H E R S T`   State   Zip Code `–`

8. Signature *(See conditions on reverse)*
Erica Nelson

OFFICIAL USE ONLY

9. Date Signed   Month   Day   Year

OFFICIAL USE ONLY
Verification Endorsement

PS Form 3575, June 1991   ☆ U.S.G.P.O. 1992-309-315

1. Item ___1___   *She was supposed to check one box.*

OR

She wasn't supposed to check two boxes.

2. Item _____

3. Item _____

4. Item _____

5. Item _____

6. Item _____

7. Item _____

8. Item _____

3 | QUESTIONS AND ANSWERS WITH *BE SUPPOSED TO*

Erica and her new husband are on their honeymoon. Complete the conversations. Use the words in the box and **be supposed to**. *Use short answers when necessary.*

~~arrive~~	be	call	do	get
land	leave	rain	shake	tip

1. ERICA: What time ___are___ we ___supposed to arrive___ in Bermuda?

   ADAM: Well, the plane _____ at 10:30, but it looks like we're

   going to be late.

2. ERICA: What time _____ we _____ to the hotel?

   ADAM: Check-in time is 12:00.

3. ERICA: _____ we _____ if we're going to be late?

   ADAM: _____. We'd better call as soon as we land.

4. ADAM: How much _____ we _____ the person who carries our

   bags for us?

   ERICA: I think it's $1.00 a bag.

5. ADAM: _____ the hotel restaurant _____ good?

   ERICA: _____. The travel agent suggested that we go somewhere else

   for dinner.

6. ERICA: What _____ we _____ with our keys when we leave

   the hotel?

   ADAM: We _____ them at the front desk.

7. ERICA: _____ it _____ today?

   ADAM: _____. But look at those clouds. I think we'd better take an

   umbrella just in case.

8. ERICA: Can you hand me that bottle of sunblock?

   ADAM: Sure. _____ you _____ the bottle before you use it?

   ERICA: I don't know. What do the instructions say?

4 | AFFIRMATIVE AND NEGATIVE STATEMENTS WITH *WAS/WERE GOING TO*

Read about Erica and Adam's plans. Write two sentences for each item. Use **was(n't)** *or* **were(n't) going to**.

1. Erica planned to be a doctor, but she became a lawyer instead.

   a. *Erica was going to be a doctor.*

   b. *She wasn't going to become a lawyer.*

2. Adam didn't plan to get married. He planned to stay single.

   a. _____

   b. _____

3. Erica and Adam planned to get married in June, but they got married in September.

   a. _____

   b. _____

4. They didn't plan to have a big wedding. They planned to have a small one.

   a. _____

   b. _____

5. They planned to live in Boston, but they moved to Amherst.

   a. _____

   b. _____

6. Adam didn't plan to change jobs. He planned to keep his old one.

   a. _____

   b. _____

5 | PERSONALIZATION

Write sentences about your own changed plans. Use **was/were supposed to** *or* **was/were going to**.

1. _____

2. _____

3. _____

4. _____

Future Possibility:
May, Might, Could

1 | AFFIRMATIVE AND NEGATIVE STATEMENTS

Read Lauren's journal entry. Complete the sentences with the words in parentheses.
Choose between affirmative and negative.

Thursday, July 3

I was supposed to go to the beach tomorrow, but the weather report says it

_____*might rain*_____. I'm not really sure what I'll do if it rains. I think I
        1. (might / rain)

_____ shopping at the mall instead. It's a holiday weekend,
        2. (may / go)

so there _____ some good sales. I really need clothes.
              3. (could / be)

I _____ find a dress for John's party. Maybe I'll call Julie.
      4. (might / be able to)

She _____ to go with me.
        5. (might / want)

  On second thought, shopping _____ such a good idea.
                                    6. (may / be)

The stores will probably be really crowded. I _____ to a
                                                    7. (could / go)

movie instead. There's a Spanish movie at Cinema 8, but I'm a little afraid that I

_____ enough of it. My Spanish really isn't that good.
      8. (might / understand)

Maybe I'll call Eric and ask him if he wants to take a drive to see Aunt Marla and

Uncle Phil. He _____ to go, though, because he doesn't like
                    9. (might / want)

driving in the rain. Oh, well. I _____ home and read a good
                                      10. (could / stay)

book. That _____ the best thing to do . . . although I really
                11. (might / be)

do need to get a new dress.

2 | CONTRAST: *BE GOING TO* OR *MIGHT*

*Read these conversations. Use **be going to** or **might** and the verbs in the box to complete the summary sentences.*

buy	call	go	have	rain
read	see	~~visit~~	work	write

1. LAUREN: Hello, Julie? This is Lauren. Do you want to go to the mall with me?

    JULIE: I don't know. I'm thinking about going to my parents'.

    SUMMARY: Julie _____ *might visit* _____ her parents.

2. JULIE: What are you looking for at the mall?

    LAUREN: I need to get a new dress for John's party.

    JULIE: Good luck! I hope you find something.

    SUMMARY: Lauren _____ a new dress.

3. LAUREN: Do you think we'll get some rain?

    CARL: Definitely. Look at those clouds.

    SUMMARY: Carl thinks it _____.

4. LAUREN: What are you doing today?

    CARL: I have tickets for a play.

    SUMMARY: Carl _____ a play.

5. LAUREN: What are you doing this weekend?

    KAYLA: I'm not sure. I'm thinking about taking a drive to the country.

    SUMMARY: Kayla _____ for a ride.

6. LAUREN: Say, Eric. Do you want to see Aunt Marla and Uncle Phil tomorrow?

    ERIC: I can't. I have to go into the office this weekend—even though it's a holiday.

    SUMMARY: Eric _____ this weekend.

7. LAUREN: How about dinner Saturday night?

    ERIC: That's an idea. Can I call and let you know tomorrow?

    LAUREN: Sure.

    SUMMARY: Lauren and Eric _____ dinner together.

8. **LAUREN:** Hi, Aunt Marla. How are you?

   MARLA: Lauren! How are you? It's good to hear your voice. Listen, we just started dinner. Can I call you back?

   LAUREN: Sure.

   MARLA: OK. I'll speak to you later.

   SUMMARY: Marla _____ Lauren later.

9. **MARLA:** Hi. It's Aunt Marla. Sorry about before. What are you doing home on a holiday weekend?

   LAUREN: I'm tired. I just want to stay home with a good book.

   SUMMARY: Lauren _____ a book.

10. **MARLA:** Do you have any other plans?

   LAUREN: Maybe I'll catch up on some of my e-mail.

   SUMMARY: Lauren _____ some e-mail.

3 | EDITING

Read Lauren's e-mail. There are four mistakes in the use of modals to express future possibility. The first mistake is already corrected. Find and correct three more.

Hi Rachel,

How are you? It's the Fourth of July, and it's raining really hard. They say it
                                                            might OR *may*
could clear up later. Then again, it ~~could~~ not. You never know with the weather.

Do you remember my brother, Eric? He says hi. He might has dinner with me

on Saturday night. We may go to a new Mexican restaurant that just opened in

the mall.

I definitely might take some vacation time next month. Perhaps we could do

something together. It might not be fun to do some traveling. What do you

think? Let me know.

Lauren

4 | PERSONALIZATION

Make a short To Do list for next weekend. Put a question mark (?) next to the things you aren't sure you'll do.

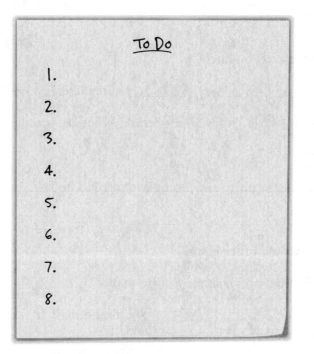

*Now write sentences about what you **are going to do** and what you **might do**.*

1. _____
2. _____
3. _____
4. _____
5. _____
6. _____
7. _____
8. _____

Conclusions: *Must, Have (got) to, May, Might, Could, Can't*

1 | AFFIRMATIVE AND NEGATIVE STATEMENTS WITH *MUST*

Read the facts. Complete the conclusions with **must** *or* **must not***.*

1. Jack is wearing a gold wedding band on his ring finger.

   CONCLUSION: He _____*must be*_____ married.
   (be)

2. You have been calling Alicia since 8:00 P.M., but no one answers the phone.

   CONCLUSION: She _____ home.
   (be)

3. Christa got 98 percent on her math test.

   CONCLUSION: Her parents _____ proud of her.
   (feel)

4. Carlos works from 9:00 to 5:00 and then attends night school.

   CONCLUSION: He _____ a lot of free time.
   (have)

5. Martin works as a mechanic in Al's Automobile Shop.

   CONCLUSION: He _____ a lot about cars.
   (know)

6. Monica owns two houses and four cars.

   CONCLUSION: She _____ a lot of money.
   (have)

7. Mr. Cantor always asks me to repeat what I say.

   CONCLUSION: He _____ well.
   (hear)

8. Chen got only four hours of sleep last night.

   CONCLUSION: He _____ very tired today.
   (feel)

(continued)

9. Carmen was born in Mexico and moved to the United States when she was 10.

   CONCLUSION: She _____ Spanish.
                                (speak)

10. Mindy never gets good grades.

    CONCLUSION: She _____ enough.
                                (study)

11. Dan just bought a bottle of aspirin and four boxes of tissues.

    CONCLUSION: He _____ a cold.
                               (have)

12. Ana and Giorgio didn't have any of the steak.

    CONCLUSION: They _____ meat.
                                (eat)

2 | CONTRAST: *MUST OR MAY / MIGHT / COULD*

Read the conversations. Circle the appropriate words.

1. **A:** Someone broke into the Petersons' house.

   B: That's terrible! What did they take?

   A: All of Mrs. Peterson's jewelry.

   B: Oh, no. She could / (must) feel awful.

   A: Is she home now?

   B: I don't know. She might / must be home. She sometimes gets home by 6:00.

2. **A:** Do the Petersons have insurance?

   B: Oh, they could / must. Mr. Peterson works at an insurance company.

3. **A:** Have you checked our burglar alarm lately?

   B: Yes. And I just put in a new battery.

   A: Good. So it must / might be OK.

4. **A:** Do you remember that guy we saw outside the Petersons' home last week?

   B: Yes. Why? Do you think he might / must be the burglar?

   A: I don't know. I guess he must / could be the burglar. He looked a little suspicious.

   B: Maybe we should tell the police about him.

5. **A:** Someone's at the door.

   B: Who <u>could / must</u> it be?

   A: I don't know.

   B: Detective Kramer wanted to ask us some questions about the burglary.

   A: Oh. It <u>must / could</u> be him. We're not expecting anybody else.

6. **A:** How old do you think Detective Kramer is?

   B: Well, he's been a detective for 10 years. So he <u>must / might</u> be at least 35.

   A: You're right. He <u>couldn't / might not</u> be much younger than 35. He probably started out as a police officer and became a detective in his mid-20s.

   B: He looks a lot younger, though.

3 | SHORT ANSWERS WITH *MUST* OR *MAY / MIGHT / COULD*

*Write a short answer to each question. Use **must** or **may/might/could** and include **be** where necessary.*

1. **A:** Is Ron a detective?

   B: _____ *He might be* _____. He always carries a notepad.

2. **A:** Does Marta speak Spanish?

   B: _____. She lived in Spain for four years.

3. **A:** Do the Taylors have a lot of money?

   B: _____. They're always taking very expensive vacations.

4. **A:** Is Ricardo married?

   B: _____. He wears a wedding ring.

5. **A:** Does Anna know Meng?

   B: _____. They both work for the same company, but it's very big.

6. **A:** Is your phone out of order?

   B: _____. It hasn't rung once today, and John always calls me by this time.

(continued)

7. **A:** Are Marcia and Scott married?

   B: _____. They both have the same last name, but it's possible that

   they're brother and sister.

8. **A:** Does Glenda drive?

   B: _____. She owns a car.

9. **A:** Is Oscar an only child?

   B: _____. I don't know. He's never mentioned a brother or sister.

10. **A:** Are the Hendersons away?

    B: _____. I haven't seen them for a week, and there are no lights on

    in their apartment.

---

4 | CONTRAST: *MIGHT, MUST, COULD, CAN'T, COULDN'T, MIGHT NOT*

Read the description of a burglary suspect and look at the four pictures. Complete the conversation with the correct words and the names of the men in the pictures.

21-year-old white male

short, curly blond hair

no scars or other

distinguishing features

Allen

Bob

Chet

Dave

DETECTIVE: Look at these four photos. It's possible that one of them

_____*could*_____ be the man we're looking for. Take your time.
     1. (must / could)

WITNESS 1: Hmmm. What do you think? _____ it be this man?
     2. (Could / Must)

WITNESS 2: It _____ be _____. He has a scar on
          3. (can't / must)   4. (Name)

his face. What about _____? He has short blond hair and
                          5. (Name)

looks 21.

WITNESS 1: I'm not sure. It _____ be. But it _____
                    6. (could / must)   7. (might / must)

also be _____. He also has blond hair and looks 21.
              8. (Name)

WITNESS 2: But he has long hair.

WITNESS 1: The photo _____ be old. Maybe he cut it.
                    9. (could / couldn't)

WITNESS 2: That's true. Well, it definitely _____ be
                              10. (couldn't / might not)

_____. He looks too old. Maybe we could look at some more
        11. (Name)

photos.

5 | PERSONALIZATION

Read the description of the burglar in Exercise 4. Look at these pictures. Is one of them the burglar? What's your opinion? Complete the sentences.

Ed   **Frank**   **George**

1. It could be _____ because _____

2. It couldn't be _____ because _____

3. It might be _____ because _____

6 | EDITING

Read this woman's journal entry. There are six mistakes in the use of modals to express conclusions. The first mistake is already corrected. Find and correct five more.

> Just got home. It's really cold outside. The temperature ~~could~~ *must* be below freezing because the walkway is all covered with ice. What a day! We went down to the police station to look at photos. They must having hundreds of photos. They kept showing us more and more. We kept looking, but it was difficult to be sure. After all, we only saw the burglar for a few seconds. They've gotta have other witnesses besides us! There were a lot of people at the mall that day. We may not be the only ones who got a look at the burglar! That's the one thing I'm certain of! In spite of our uncertainty with the photos, the detective was very patient. I guess he must be used to witnesses like us. Nevertheless, it have to be frustrating for him. I know the police may really want to catch this guy.

Workbook Answer Key

In this answer key, where the contracted form is given, the full form is often also correct, and where the full form is given, the contracted form is often also correct.

UNIT 1 (pages 1–8)

1

2. getting, gets
3. giving, gives
4. grabbing, grabs
5. having, has
6. planning, plans
7. saying, says
8. starting, starts
9. trying, tries
10. watching, watches

2

2. drives
3. takes
4. isn't taking
5. 's taking
6. are repairing
7. is using
8. doesn't . . . use
9. takes
10. moves
11. is slowing down
12. 's raining
13. doesn't like
14. drives
15. is listening
16. listens
17. is describing
18. isn't moving
19. hates
20. doesn't want
21. feels
22. knows
23. is

3

Answers will vary.

4

Postcard A

2. 'm standing
3. is getting
4. looks
5. rains
6. has
7. 's taking
8. 's starting

Postcard B

1. love
2. 'm studying
3. living
4. is improving
5. speak
6. 're helping
7. want
8. miss

5

3. Aldo and Emilia (OR They) go to school.
4. Aldo and Emilia (OR They) are having lunch.
5. Aldo works at the bookstore. Emilia studies at the library.
6. Aldo plays soccer. Emilia plays basketball.
7. Aldo is going home. Emilia is doing homework at the library.
8. Aldo has dinner. Emilia practices the guitar.
9. Aldo does homework. Emilia has dinner.
10. Aldo is playing computer games. Emilia is watching TV.

6

2. Aldo doesn't watch TV. He reads the newspaper.
3. Emilia doesn't work at the bookstore. Aldo works at the bookstore. (OR She studies at the library.)
4. Emilia isn't playing tennis. She's playing basketball.
5. They don't always have dinner together. Aldo has dinner at 6:00. Emilia has dinner at 7:00.

7

2. A: When do Aldo and Emilia get up?
   B: They get up at 7:30.
3. A: Does Emilia walk in the morning?
   B: No, she doesn't.
4. A: What are they doing now?
   B: They're having lunch.
5. A: Is Aldo doing homework now?
   B: No, he isn't.
6. A: Does Emilia do her homework at school?
   B: No, she doesn't.
7. A: When does Emilia play basketball?
   B: (She plays basketball) At 4:00.
8. A: Does Aldo play computer games before dinner?
   B: No, he doesn't.

8

2. Emilia is usually on time.
3. Aldo and Emilia never miss school.
4. These days they're studying English. OR They're studying English these days.
5. They usually speak Italian.
6. Now they're speaking English. OR They're speaking English now.
7. Aldo and Emilia always do their homework.
8. Aldo is often tired.
9. The students usually eat lunch in school.
10. They're always hungry.
11. At the moment Emilia is having a snack. OR Emilia is having a snack at the moment.
12. Emilia rarely goes to bed late.

9

How are you? ~~I write~~ *I'm writing* you this e-mail before my class.

I ~~am having~~ *have* a part-time job as a clerk in the mail room of a small company. The pay isn't good, but ~~I'm liking~~ *I like* the people there. They're all friendly, and we ~~are speaking~~ *speak* Spanish all the time. I'm also taking Spanish classes at night at a language institute. The class ~~is meeting~~ *meets* three times a week. It just started last week, so ~~I'm not knowing~~ *I don't know* many of the other students yet. They seem nice, though.

~~I'm thinking~~ *I think* that I'm beginning to get accustomed to living here. At first I experienced some "culture shock." I understand that this is quite normal. But these days ~~I meet~~ *I'm meeting* more and more people because of my job and my class, so I'm feeling more connected to things.

What ~~do you do~~ *are you doing* these days? ~~Do you still look~~ *Are you still looking* for a new job?

Please write when you can. ~~I'm always liking~~ *I always like* to hear from you.

10

Answers will vary.

UNIT 2 (pages 9–11)

1

3. Don't lean backward.
4. Take a small step.
5. Don't breathe in.
6. Count slowly.
7. Don't speak loudly.
8. Keep your eyes shut.
9. Don't wear tight clothes.
10. Wear a white T-shirt.
11. Wear light clothes.
12. Don't turn the lights off.
13. Turn the music up.
14. Put the heat on low.
15. Don't come late.
16. Don't lock the bottom lock.

2

3.	Walk	10.	Continue
4.	ride	11.	stop
5.	Show	12.	Don't cross
6.	Give	13.	be
7.	Go	14.	Don't pass
8.	Don't turn	15.	Have
9.	make	16.	Don't work

3

Your mother called. ~~Calls~~ *Call* her at your sister's tonight.
Don't ~~you~~ call after 10:00, though.
I went to the gym.

Please wash*
~~Wash please~~ the dishes and ~~threw~~ *throw* out the trash.
^

take
If anyone calls for me, ~~takes~~ a message.

have
Thanks a lot and ~~has~~ a good evening!

*OTHER POSSIBLE CORRECTIONS: Wash the dishes, please, and throw out the trash. OR Wash the dishes and throw out the trash, please.

4

Answers will vary.

UNIT 3 (pages 12–18)

1

2. began	**17.** met
3. bought	**18.** moved
4. caught	**19.** needed
5. came	**20.** opened
6. died	**21.** put
7. did	**22.** read
8. felt	**23.** said
9. found	**24.** saw
10. got	**25.** took
11. gave	**26.** thought
12. had	**27.** understood
13. hurried	**28.** voted
14. kissed	**29.** won
15. lived	**30.** wrote
16. looked	**31.** was, were

2

2. was	**7.** was, wasn't
3. weren't, were	**8.** wasn't, was
4. wasn't	**9.** were
5. was	**10.** were
6. wasn't, was	

3

2. A: Where was Simone de Beauvoir from?
  B: She was from France.
3. A: What nationality was Pablo Neruda?
  B: He was Chilean.
4. A: Who was Boccaccio?
  B: He was a poet and storyteller.
5. A: Was Agatha Christie French?
  B: No, she wasn't.
6. A: What nationality was Lucy M. Montgomery?
  B: She was Canadian.
7. A: Was Nazim Hikmet a poet?
  B: Yes, he was.

8. A: When was Karel Čapek born?
  B: He was born in 1890.
9. A: Who was Isaak Babel?
  B: He was a short-story writer and playwright.

4

Biography A

2. grew up	**6.** used
3. taught	**7.** wrote
4. began	**8.** moved
5. loved	**9.** died

Biography B

1. was	**6.** taught
2. planned	**7.** loved
3. began	**8.** married
4. painted	**9.** had
5. studied	**10.** died

Biography C

1. were	**4.** watched
2. built	**5.** took place
3. flew	**6.** lasted

5

2. A: Where did he grow up?
  B: He grew up in Hungary.
3. A: What did he do?
  B: He was a composer. OR He wrote music.
4. A: Did he spend his whole life in Hungary?
  B: No, he didn't.
5. A: Did Frida Kahlo plan to be a painter?
  B: No, she didn't.
6. A: When did she begin painting?
  B: She began painting after a serious accident.
7. A: What did she paint?
  B: She painted pictures of her family and friends. She also painted pictures of herself.
8. A: When did she die?
  B: She died in 1954.
9. A: Where did the Wright brothers build their first planes?
  B: (They built their first planes) in their bicycle shop in Ohio.
10. A: Did both brothers fly the *Flyer 1*?
  B: No, they didn't.
11. A: Where did the first controlled flight take place?
  B: (It took place) near Kitty Hawk, North Carolina.
12. A: How long did the flight last?
  B: (It lasted) only about 12 seconds.

6

3. Orville didn't have serious health problems.
4. Wilbur didn't grow a moustache.
5. Orville didn't lose most of his hair.
6. Wilbur didn't take courses in Latin.
7. Wilbur didn't like to play jokes.
8. Wilbur didn't dress very fashionably.
9. Wilbur didn't play the guitar.
10. Orville didn't build the first glider.
11. Orville didn't make the first attempts to fly.
12. Orville didn't choose the location of Kitty Hawk.
13. Wilbur didn't have a lot of patience.
14. Wilbur didn't live a long life.

7

was
Pablo Neruda (1904–1973) ~~were~~ a famous poet, political activist, and diplomat. He was
went
born in Parral, Chile. When he was 17 he ~~gone~~ to Santiago to continue his education. He did
finish
not ~~finished~~, but he soon published his first book.
spent
first book. Neruda ~~spends~~ the next several decades traveling and continuing to write poetry. In 1971, while he was Chile's ambassador to
won
France, he ~~winned~~ the Nobel Prize in literature.
died
He ~~dead~~ two years later.

UNIT 4 (pages 19–23)

1

2. wasn't writing
3. was answering
4. were eating
5. weren't eating
6. was attending
7. weren't writing
8. were discussing
9. wasn't answering
10. was returning

2

2. A: What was he doing at 9:30?
   B: He was meeting with Ms. Jacobs.
3. A: Was Mr. Cotter writing police reports at 10:30?
   B: No, he wasn't.
4. A: What kind of reports was he writing?
   B: He was writing financial reports.
5. A: What was he doing at 11:30?
   B: He was answering correspondence.
6. A: Was he having lunch at 12:00?
   B: Yes, he was.
7. A: Who was eating lunch with him?
   B: Mr. Webb was eating lunch with him.
8. A: Where were they having lunch?
   B: They were having lunch at Sol's Cafe.
9. A: Who was he talking to at 3:30?
   B: He was talking to Alan.
10. A: What were they discussing?
    B: They were discussing the budget.

3

2. was crossing
3. was speeding
4. didn't stop
5. was
6. saw
7. was walking
8. saw
9. noticed
10. was going
11. reached
12. went
13. hit
14. took out
15. called
16. didn't stop
17. happened
18. came
19. got
20. was lying
21. was bleeding
22. was
23. were questioning
24. said
25. was crossing
26. went
27. knocked
28. happened
29. had
30. was crossing
31. didn't see
32. broke
33. had
34. were not

4

2. What did you do when you heard the noise?
3. What did you see when you looked in the direction of the sound?
4. Where were you standing when you saw the Honda?
5. Did the driver stop when the accident occurred?
6. What happened next?
7. Did you get a look at the driver while he was driving away?
8. What was the victim doing when the car hit her?

UNIT 5 (pages 24–26)

1

2. People used to read
3. People used to cook
4. People used to wash
5. People used to use
6. It used to take

2

2. didn't use to work
3. didn't use to have
4. used to take
5. didn't use to be
6. used to live
7. didn't use to like
8. didn't use to know
9. used to return
10. used to make

3

2. A: Where did she use to live?
  B: She used to live in New York.
3. A: Did she use to live in a house?
  B: No, she didn't.
4. A: What did she use to do?
  B: She used to be a student.
5. A: Which school did she use to attend?
  B: She used to attend City College.
6. A: Did she use to have long hair?
  B: Yes, she did.
7. A: Did she use to wear glasses?
  B: No, she didn't.
8. A: Did she use to be married?
  B: Yes, she did.

4

　　Today I ran into an old classmate. We used to be in the same science class. In fact, we used to ~~studied~~ *study* together for tests. He was a very good student, and he always ~~uses~~ *used* to get A's. At first I almost didn't recognize Jason! He looked so different. He used to ~~had~~ *have* very dark hair. Now he's almost all gray. He also used to ~~being~~ *be* a little heavy. Now he's quite thin. And he was wearing a suit and tie! I couldn't believe it. He never ~~use~~ *used* to dress that way. He only used to ~~wore~~ *wear* jeans! His personality seemed different, too. He didn't ~~used~~ *use* to talk very much. Now he seems very outgoing. I wonder what he thought of me! I'm sure I look and act different from the way I ~~was~~ used to too!

5

Answers will vary.

UNIT 6 (pages 27–34)

1

2. She's going to wash the car.
3. They're going to get gas.
4. She's going to make a left turn.
5. She's going to get a ticket.
6. They're going to crash.
7. They're going to eat lunch.
8. It's going to rain.

2

2. How long are you going to stay?
3. Are you going to stay at a hotel?
4. What are you going to do in San Francisco?
5. Are you going to visit Fisherman's Wharf?
6. Is your daughter going to go with you?
7. What is he going to do?
8. When are you going to leave?

3

2. He isn't going to take the train.
　　He's going to fly OR take a plane.
3. He isn't going to travel alone.
　　He's going to travel with his wife.
4. They aren't going to leave from Chicago.
　　They're going to leave from New York City.
5. They aren't going to fly US Airways.
　　They're going to fly FairAir.
6. They aren't going to leave on July 11.
　　They're going to leave on June 11.
7. They aren't going to take Flight 149.
　　They're going to take Flight 194.
8. It isn't going to depart at 7:00 A.M.
　　It's going to depart at 7:00 P.M.
9. They aren't going to sit apart.
　　They're going to sit together.
10. She isn't going to sit in Seat 15B.
　　She's going to sit in Seat 15C.

4

2. will become
3. Will . . . replace
4. won't replace
5. will . . . operate
6. will . . . do
7. 'll be
8. 'll sing
9. 'll dance
10. Will . . . tell
11. will
12. won't . . . be
13. will . . . do
14. Will . . . have
15. will
16. will . . . help
17. 'll replace
18. 'll perform
19. won't be
20. will improve
21. will lose
22. will create
23. Will . . . need
24. will . . . look
25. won't look
26. 'll resemble
27. will . . . happen
28. 'll happen

5

Next Wednesday <u>is</u> the first performance of *Robots*. Melissa Robins <u>is playing</u> the leading role. Robins, who lives in Italy and who is vacationing in Greece, is not available for an interview at this time. She <u>is</u>, however, <u>appearing</u> on Channel 8's "Theater Talk" sometime next month.

Although shows traditionally begin at 8:00 P.M., *Robots*, because of its length, <u>starts</u> half an hour earlier.

Immediately following the opening-night performance, the company <u>is having</u> a reception in the theater lounge. Tickets are still available. Call 555-6310 for more information.

6

2. I'm going to do
3. I'll ask
4. it's going to rain
5. They're showing
6. we're going to have
7. it's going to spill, I'll be
8. I'll take
9. We're going to arrive
10. are we going to get
11. We'll take, will still be
12. We're landing
13. are you going to stay
14. we'll see

7

I'm going
~~I going~~ to stay here for a week with my parents.

We have a lot of fun things planned.
we're seeing OR *we're going to see*
Tomorrow night ~~we'll see~~ a play called *Robots*. Mom already bought the tickets for it. The play
we're having OR *we're going to have*
begins at 7:30, and before that ~~we have~~ dinner on Fisherman's Wharf. Right now we're sitting in Golden Gate Park, but we have to leave. The sky
's going to
is getting very dark. It ~~will~~ rain!
'll call
I ~~call~~ you soon.

8

Answers will vary.

UNIT 7 (pages 35–38)

1

2. gets up . . . 'll take (i)
3. is . . . 'll drink (c)
4. eat . . . 'll read (j)
5. finish . . . 'll do (g)
6. washes . . . 'll dry (e)
7. get in . . . 'll fasten (d)
8. gets . . . 'll drive (b)
9. stops . . . 'll need (f)
10. is . . . 'll be (a)

2

2. will apply (OR 's going to apply) . . . before . . . finishes
3. After . . . finishes . . . 'll visit (OR 's going to visit)
4. While . . . works . . . 'll take (OR 's going to take)
5. 'll visit (OR 's going to visit) . . . before . . . gets
6. When . . . finishes . . . 'll fly (OR 's going to fly)
7. 'll get married (OR 's going to get married) . . . when . . . 's
8. 'll return (OR 's going to return) . . . after . . . gets married
9. 'll move (OR 's going to move) . . . when . . . returns
10. After . . . moves . . . 'll look for (OR 's going to look for)

3

2. Vera saves enough money from her job, she's going to buy a plane ticket.
3. Vera goes home, she's going to buy presents for her family.
4. Vera arrives at the airport, her father will be there to drive her home.
5. Vera and her father get home, they'll have dinner.
6. Vera will give her family the presents . . . they finish dinner.
7. Vera's brother will wash the dishes . . . Vera's sister dries them.
8. The whole family will stay up talking . . . the clock strikes midnight.
9. they go to bed, they'll all feel very tired.
10. Vera will fall asleep . . . her head hits the pillow.
11. Vera wakes up the next morning, she'll call her friends.
12. She'll see her friends . . . she has breakfast.

4

I'm really looking forward to your arrival tomorrow. Before you ~~will~~ know it, you'll be here! After I ~~will~~ pick you up at the airport, we'll go straight to my parents' house. My mother is going to make a special dinner, but before we have

dinner, you and I ~~go~~ *will go* for a drive with Paulo. Rio is a beautiful city, and we can't wait to show you some of the sights. After we ~~will~~ have dinner*,* some ^

of our friends will come over to meet you.

Let's talk on the phone once more*,* before

~~you're going to leave~~ *you leave*. I'm going out for a few

hours, but ~~I call~~ *I'll call* you as soon as I get back. I'll speak to you soon.

5

Answers will vary.

UNIT 8 (pages 39–45)

1

2. Whose phone rang at midnight?
3. Who was calling for Michelle?
4. Who was having a party?
5. How many people left the party?
6. What surprised them?
7. Whose friend called the police?
8. How many police arrived?
9. What happened next?
10. Who told the police about a theft?
11. Whose jewelry disappeared?
12. How many necklaces vanished?

2

2. How many rooms does her apartment have? (f)
3. How much rent does she pay? (j)
4. When does she pay the rent? (c)
5. Who does she live with? (h)
6. What does she do? (g)
7. Which company does she work for? (d)
8. How long does she plan to stay there? (a)
9. How does she get to work? (b)
10. Why does she take the bus? (i)

3

2. Why did you leave Chicago?
3. Who moved with you?
4. Where did you get a job?
5. When did it start?
6. How many rooms does it have?

7. How many of the rooms came with carpeting?
8. How much do you each pay?
9. What do you need to buy?
10. Whose brother wants to visit her?
11. Who called last Sunday?
12. Who did you speak to?
13. When do they want to visit you?
14. Why is there plenty of room?

4

Answers will vary.

UNIT 9 (pages 43–45)

1

2. himself
3. themselves
4. itself
5. herself
6. yourself, yourselves OR yourselves, yourself
7. themselves
8. itself
9. themselves
10. ourselves

2

2. each other
3. herself
4. themselves
5. each other's
6. herself
7. yourselves
8. itself
9. ourselves
10. each other

3

2. are criticizing each other OR one another
3. is going to help himself
4. are talking to themselves
5. are introducing themselves OR one another
6. are talking to each other
7. drove herself
8. blames OR is blaming himself
9. are enjoying each other's OR one another's
10. are thanking each other OR one another

4

I really enjoyed ~~me~~ *myself* at Gina's party! Hank was there and we talked to ~~ourselves~~ *each other OR one another* quite a bit. He's a little depressed about losing his job. The job ~~himself~~ *itself* wasn't that great, but he needs the money. He's disappointed in himself. He thinks it's all his own fault, and he blames ~~him~~ *himself* for the whole thing.

Hank introduced ~~myself~~ *me* to several of his friends. I spoke a lot to this one woman, Cara. We have a lot of things in common, and after just an hour, we felt like we had known ~~each other's~~ *each other* forever. Cara, ~~himself~~ *herself*, is a computer programmer, just like me.

At first I was nervous about going to the party alone. I sometimes feel a little uncomfortable when I'm in a social situation by ~~oneself~~ *myself*. But this time was different. Before I went, I kept telling myself to relax. My roommate, too, kept telling ~~myself~~ *me*, "Don't be so hard on ~~you~~ *yourself*! Just have fun!" That's what I advised Hank to do too. Before we left the party, Hank and I promised ~~us~~ *each other* OR *one another* to keep in touch. I hope to see him again soon.

UNIT 10 (pages 46–50)

1

2. out	11. out
3. on	12. up
4. off	13. out
5. back	14. in
6. out	15. out
7. down	16. back
8. out	17. together
9. up	18. over
10. up	

2

2. Pick out, help . . . out	6. Look . . . over
3. look up	7. Do . . . over
4. Set up, talk over	8. Hand . . . in
5. Write up	

3

2. clean it up	6. turn it down
3. call her back	7. hand them in
4. turn it down	8. drop it off
5. wake him up	

4

2. Point out common mistakes. OR Point common mistakes out.
3. Talk them over.
4. Pick out a new problem. OR Pick a new problem out.
5. Work it out with the class.
6. Write the results up. OR Write up the results.
7. Go on to the next unit.
8. Make up the final exam questions. OR Make the final exam questions up.
9. Hand them out.

10. Set up study groups. OR Set study groups up.
11. Help them out.
12. Call off Friday's class. OR Call Friday's class off.

5

How are things going? I'm already into the second month of the spring semester, and I've got a lot of work to do. For science class, I have to write a term paper. The professor made ~~over~~ *up* a list of possible topics. After looking ~~over them~~ *them over*, I think I've picked one out. I'm going to write about chimpanzees. I've already looked *up* some information about them online ~~up~~ ^. I found ~~up~~ *out* some very interesting facts.

Did you know that their hands look very much like their feet, and that they have fingernails and toenails? Their thumbs and big toes are "opposable." This makes it easy for them to pick things ~~out~~ *up* with both their fingers and toes. Their arms are longer than their legs. This helps ~~out them~~ *them out*, too, because they can reach out to fruit growing on thin branches that would not otherwise support their weight. Adult males weigh between 90 and 115 pounds, and they are about four feet high when they stand ~~out~~ *up*.

Like humans, chimpanzees are very social. They travel in groups called "communities." Mothers bring ~~out~~ *up* their chimps, who stay with them until about the age of seven. Even after the chimps grow up, there is still a lot of contact with other chimpanzees.

I could go on, but I need to stop writing now so I can clean ~~out~~ *up* my room (it's a mess!) a little before going to bed. It's late already, and I have to get ~~early up~~ *up early* tomorrow morning for my 9:00 class.

Please let me know how you are. Or call me. I'm often out, but if you leave a message, I'll call ~~back you~~ *you back* as soon as I can. It would be great to speak to you.

UNIT 11 (pages 51–58)

1

3. can read an English newspaper . . . could (read one)
4. couldn't read an English novel . . . can't (read one)

5. can speak on the phone . . . couldn't (speak on the phone)

6. couldn't speak with a group of people . . . can (speak with a group of people)

7. could write an e-mail . . . can (write one)

8. Before the course, he couldn't write a business letter, and he still can't (write one).

9. Now he can order a meal in English, and he could (order a meal in English) before too.

10. Now he can go shopping, and he could (go shopping) before too.

SUMMARY: can . . . could

2

2. A: What languages can you speak?

3. A: Could you speak Spanish when you were a child?

B: No, I couldn't.

4. A: Could you speak French?

B: Yes, I could.

5. A: Before you came here, could you understand spoken English?

B: No, I couldn't.

6. A: Can you understand song lyrics?

B: Yes, I can.

7. A: Before this course, could you write a business letter in English?

B: No, I couldn't.

8. A: Could you drive a car before you came here?

B: No, I couldn't.

9. A: Can you drive a car now?

B: No, I can't.

10. A: Can you swim?

B: Yes, I can.

11. A: Could you surf before you came here?

B: No, I couldn't.

12. A: What can you do now that you couldn't do before?

B: can do . . . couldn't do

3

2. are able to interpret

3. are not able to distinguish

4. are not able to understand

5. are able to hear

6. are able to get back

7. are able to read

8. is not able to recognize

9. is not able to work

10. are able to communicate

4

3. How will . . . be able to see

4. Will . . . be able to hear

5. No, you won't.

6. How will . . . be able to solve

7. Will . . . be able to enjoy

8. Yes, you will.

5

2. could read

3. could not OR couldn't accept

4. was able to accept

5. could see

6. will . . . be able to do

7. can do

8. can do

9. can speak

10. was able to achieve

11. will be able to get

12. can read

13. can change

14. can do

6

Before I came to this country, I ~~can't~~ *couldn't* do many things in English. For example, I couldn't follow a conversation if many people were talking at the same time. I remember a party I went to. Everyone was speaking English, and I wasn't able ^*to* understand a word! I felt so uncomfortable. Finally, my aunt came to pick me up, and I ~~could~~ *was able to* leave the party.

Today I can ✗ understand much better. I am taking classes at the adult center. My teacher is very good. She can ~~explains~~ *explain* things well, and she always gives us the chance to talk a lot in class. When I finish this class, I ~~can~~ *will be able to* speak and understand a lot better.

~~Be~~ *Being* able to speak English well is very important to me. I practice a lot at home too. When I first came to this country, I ~~can't~~ *couldn't OR wasn't able to* understand very much TV, but now I can ✗ understand much better. In fact, I can do a lot now, and I think in a few more months I ~~can~~ *'ll be able to* ^ do even more.

7

Answers will vary.

UNIT 12 (pages 59–62)

1

2. c **6.** a
3. b **7.** e
4. h **8.** g
5. f

2

2. we (please) review Unit 6? OR we review Unit 6, please?
3. I (please) borrow your pen? OR I borrow your pen, please?
4. I look at your (class) notes?
5. I come late to the next class?
6. my roommate (please) come to the next class with me? OR my roommate come to the next class with me, please?
7. I (please) ask a question? OR I ask a question, please?
8. we (please) use a dictionary? OR we use a dictionary, please?
9. we (please) leave five minutes early? OR we leave five minutes early, please?
10. my sister goes on the class trip with the rest of the class?

3

Answers will vary.

4

2. can bring **7.** may not pay
3. can bring **8.** may not purchase
4. can't OR cannot drink **9.** can't OR cannot get
5. can pay **10.** may swim
6. can pay

5

I've been sick for the past two days. That's why I
take
missed the last test. May I ~~taking~~ a make-up exam?
Yes. If you bring a doctor's note.
If I can take the exam, may I use my calculator during the test?
may not
No, you ~~mayn't~~! I did not allow calculators during this test.
come
Could my roommate ~~comes~~ to class and take notes for me on Thursday?
can
Yes, he ~~could~~.
if
Do you mind ~~when~~ he records the class for me?
Not at all. It's fine for him to record the class.
One last thing—I know I missed some handouts.

please have
May I ~~have please~~ copies of them?
Sure. I'll give them to your roommate on Thursday.
Thanks a lot.

UNIT 13 (pages 63–67)

1

2. a **7.** b
3. h **8.** i
4. g **9.** f
5. j **10.** e
6. c

"Yes" responses: 2, 4, 5, 6, 7, 9, 10
"No" responses: 1, 3, 8
Negative = "OK": 5

2

2. opening the window
3. buy some stamps
4. pick up a sandwich
5. staying late tonight
6. keep the noise down
7. come to my office
8. get Frank's phone number
9. explaining this note to me
10. lend me $5.00

3

2. Would you mind working on Saturday?
3. Will you please help me? OR Will you help me, please?
4. Would you please explain this? OR Would you explain this, please?
5. Could you please drive me home? OR Could you drive me home, please?

4

(Note 3) Will you return please the stapler? → Will you please return the stapler? OR Will you return the stapler, please?
(Note 5) Would you mind leave → Would you mind leaving
(Note 6) Could you please remember to lock the door. → Could you please remember to lock the door?
(Note 7) Would you please to call Ms. Rivera before the end of the day? → Would you please call Ms. Rivera before the end of the day? OR Would you call Ms. Rivera before the end of the day, please?
(Note 8) Also, would you mind to e-mail Lisa Barker a copy? → Also, would you mind e-mailing Lisa Barker a copy?

5

Answers will vary.

UNIT 14 (pages 68–72)

1

2. You shouldn't shout into the phone.
3. You should speak in a quiet, normal voice.
4. You should leave the room to make a phone call.
5. You shouldn't discuss private issues in public places.
6. You shouldn't stand too close to other people when you are talking on the phone.
7. You should pay attention to other people on the street when you are walking and talking.
8. You shouldn't dial while you are driving. OR You should never dial while you are driving.

2

2. should call
3. 'd better not forget
4. a. ought to see
   b. 'd better buy
5. should try
6. a. ought to think
   b. should look into
7. a. shouldn't talk
   b. should be
8. 'd better not call
9. ought to have
10. should get
11. shouldn't talk
12. 'd better hang up

3

3. What should I wear?
4. Should I bring a gift?
5. No, you shouldn't.
6. Should I bring something to eat or drink?
7. You should bring something to drink.
8. When should I respond?
9. You should respond by May 15.
10. Should I call Aunt Rosa?
11. No, you shouldn't.
12. Who should I call?
13. You should call Amy and leave a message at 555-3234.

4

Party Etiquette Quiz
Do you know what you should do at a party?
Check the best answer.

1. You are at a party and you can't remember someone's name. What ~~you should~~ *should you* do?
   ☐ a. You should ~~no~~ *not* ask the person's name.
   ☐ b. ~~You better~~ *You'd better* leave immediately!
   ☐ c. You ought *to* just ask.

2. You don't know anyone at the party, and your host doesn't introduce you to the other guests. ~~Had you better~~ *Should you* introduce yourself?
   ☐ a. Yes, you should. You should say "Hi. My name's _____."
   ☐ b. No, you ~~should~~ *shouldn't*. You'd better tell the host to introduce you.

3. Your cell phone rings during the party. ~~You should~~ *Should you* answer it?
   ☐ a. Just let it ring. You ~~had not better~~ *'d better not* answer it.
   ☐ b. You should answer it, but just have a short conversation.
   ☐ c. You really ought to leave the room and speak to the person in private.

4. You had a very nice time at the party. How ~~you should~~ *should you* thank your host?
   ☐ a. You should just say "thank you" when you leave.
   ☐ b. You should send a "thank you" e-mail the next day.
   ☐ c. You ~~oughta~~ *ought to* write a long "thank you" letter and send a gift too.

5

Answers will vary.

UNIT 15 (pages 73–76)

1

2. a
3. b
4. g
5. j
6. e
7. i
8. f
9. d
10. h

2

2. Maybe you could / .
3. Let's / .
4. How about / ?
5. Why don't you / ?
6. Let's / .
7. Maybe we could / .
8. Why doesn't she / ?
9. Why don't you / ?
10. How about / ?
11. Maybe we could / .
12. That's a good idea / .

3

2. take the "T"
3. go to Haymarket
4. taking an elevator to the top of the John Hancock Observatory
5. take a boat excursion
6. going to the New England Aquarium
7. eat at Legal Sea Foods
8. walk along the waterfront
9. going shopping in Downtown Crossing
10. walk the Freedom Trail

4

Answers will vary.

UNIT 16 (pages 77–80)

1

2. brought
3. come
4. eaten
5. fallen
6. gotten
7. had
8. looked
9. lost
10. played
11. watched
12. won

2

2. since
3. since
4. for
5. Since
6. For
7. for
8. since

3

Biography A
2. since
3. Since
4. has gone on
5. For
6. have seen
7. Since
8. has earned
9. (has) broken

Biography B
1. has been
2. for
3. Since
4. has won
5. has become
6. has dreamed OR has dreamt
7. since
8. Since
9. has continued

4

2. A: How long has he been a professional golfer?
   B: (He's been a professional golfer) since he was 16. OR for _____ years.
3. A: Has he won any major tournaments since he turned professional?
   B: Yes, he has.
4. A: How long has he been in TV commercials?
   B: (He has been in TV commercials) for the past few years.
5. A: How long has Michelle Kwan been a skater?
   B: (She has been a skater) since she was five. OR for more than twenty years.
6. A: How many World Competitions has she won since 1986?
   B: She has won five.
7. A: Has she gotten an Olympic gold medal since she began competing?
   B: No, she hasn't.
8. A: Has she skated again since the Olympics?
   B: Yes, she has.

5

3. Min Ho has won three awards
4. Marilyn has entered two competitions
5. Victor and Marilyn haven't seen each other since 1998.
6. Karl has been a golfer since 1999.
7. Karl has lost three tournaments
8. Andreas hasn't been to (OR gone to) a tennis match

UNIT 17 (pages 81–84)

1

2. become
3. danced
4. drunk
5. fought
6. given
7. held
8. kept
9. known
10. sung
11. smiled
12. traveled

2

2. 've already looked
3. haven't found . . . yet
4. 've already seen
5. haven't gone . . . yet
6. 've already wasted
7. Have . . . decided . . . yet
8. haven't made up . . . yet

3

3. Has she bought two bookcases yet? Yes, she's already bought two bookcases.

4. Has she thrown away old magazines yet? No, she hasn't thrown away old magazines yet. OR No, she hasn't yet thrown away old magazines.

5. Has she found a painter yet? No, she hasn't found a painter yet. OR No, she hasn't yet found a painter.

6. Has she collected boxes for packing yet? Yes, she's already collected boxes for packing.

7. Has she bought a new couch yet? No, she hasn't bought a new couch yet. OR No, she hasn't yet bought a new couch.

8. Has she given away the old couch yet? Yes, she's already given away the old couch.

9. Has she cleaned the refrigerator and stove yet? No, she hasn't cleaned the refrigerator and stove yet. OR No, she hasn't yet cleaned the refrigerator and stove.

10. Has she made a list of cleaning supplies yet? Yes, she's already made a list of cleaning supplies.

11. Has she gotten a change-of-address form from the post office yet? Yes, she's already gotten a change-of-address form from the post office.

12. Has she invited the neighbors over for a goodbye party yet? No, she hasn't invited the neighbors over for a goodbye party yet. OR No, she hasn't yet invited the neighbors over for a goodbye party.

4

I'm writing to you from our new apartment! We've already ~~be~~ *been* here two weeks, and we feel very much at home. But there's still a lot to do. Believe it or not, we haven't unpacked all the boxes ~~already~~ *yet*! We took most of our old furniture, so we don't need to get too much new stuff. We had to buy a new couch for the living room, but they haven't delivered it yet.

We've already ~~meet~~ *met* some of our new neighbors. They seem very nice. One of them ~~have~~ *has* already invited us over for coffee.

~~Had~~ *Have* you made vacation plans yet? As soon as we get the couch (it's a sleeper), we'd love for you to visit. ~~Already we've planned~~ *We've already planned* places to take you when you come!

1

2. decided	**8.** ridden
3. flown	**9.** seen
4. gone	**10.** swum
5. heard	**11.** traveled
6. kept	**12.** worked
7. made	

2

2. 've ridden
3. 've heard
4. 've seen
5. 's flown
6. 've swum
7. has decided
8. 's worked

3

2. have appeared
3. have . . . loved
4. have not stopped
5. has written
6. (has) contributed
7. have . . . received
8. has described
9. has introduced
10. has included
11. has given
12. has not been
13. has been
14. have done
15. have produced
16. has . . . encouraged
17. haven't read

4

2. How many times have you visited, I've visited Europe more than 10 times.

3. Have you ever been, I've recently been on an African safari.

4. Have you ever been, Yes, I've been to Costa Rica.

5. How often have you been, I've been there once.

6. Have you (ever) traveled, I've never traveled in China.

7. Have you ever gone up, I've never gone up in a hot-air balloon.

8. Have you ever swum, I've swum with dolphins many times.

9. Have you ever taken, I've never taken a group tour.

5

Answers will vary.

UNIT 19 (pages 89–93)

1

3. Tom has gone
4. Tom got
5. Tom has made
6. Tom met
7. Tom has been
8. Tom looked
9. Tom bought
10. Tom has paid
11. Tom has read
12. Tom has taken
13. Tom has given
14. Tom felt

2

2. got
3. 've been
4. did . . . have
5. became
6. had
7. were
8. did . . . last
9. divorced
10. Did . . . have
11. didn't
12. 've remained
13. saw
14. have become
15. Has . . . remarried
16. hasn't
17. did . . . fail
18. got
19. didn't know
20. did . . . meet
21. were
22. did . . . move
23. 've lived

3

2. began
3. got
4. had
5. was
6. has risen
7. occurred
8. has created
9. started
10. had
11. were
12. has . . . increased
13. stayed
14. got
15. has changed
16. has reached

4

    met
Last month, I ~~have met~~ the most wonderful
guy. His name is Roger, and he is a student in my
    's lived
night class. He ~~lived~~ here since 1992. Before that
he lived in Detroit too, so we have a lot in
    was
common. Roger ~~has been~~ married for five years
but got divorced last April.
    have spent
    Roger and I ~~spent~~ a lot of time together. Last
    we've
week I saw him every night, and this week ~~we~~
already gotten together three times after class.
    saw
Monday night we ~~have seen~~ a great movie.
Have you seen
~~Did you see~~ *The Purple Room*? It's playing at all
the theaters.

    We've decided to take a trip back to Detroit in
the summer. Maybe we can get together. It would
be great to see you again. Please let me know if
you'll be there.

                    I took
P.S. Here's a photo of Roger that ~~I've taken~~ a few
weeks ago.

5

Answers will vary.

UNIT 20 (pages 94–98)

1

2. She's been writing articles about elephants
   since last month OR for a month.
3. Amanda and Pete haven't been living in New
   York since a few years ago OR for a few years.
4. They've been living in London since 2004 OR
   for _____ years.
5. Pete hasn't been selling books since last year
   OR for a year.
6. Pete and Amanda have been thinking of
   opening their own business since last year OR
   for a year.
7. Pete has been studying economics since last
   month OR for a month OR since he went back
   to school (last month).
8. Amanda and Pete have been looking for a new
   apartment since a month ago OR for a month.

2

2. has been selling
3. has been fighting
4. have opened
5. has . . . done
6. has been
7. has been traveling
8. has received
9. has been working
10. has written
11. has . . . been combining
12. has changed

3

2. have . . . been
3. have . . . been doing
4. 've been reading
5. Have . . . read
6. 've seen
7. Have . . . bought
8. 've been using
9. has . . . opened
10. 've been opening

4

2. How long has she been a businesswoman?
3. How much money has her business made this year?
4. How long has she been traveling around the world?
5. How many countries has she visited?
6. Have her shops been opening in Asia? OR Have her shops opened in Asia?
7. How many copies of her book has she sold?
8. Has she written any books since *Business as Unusual*?
9. How many awards has she won?
10. What has she been working on these days?
11. How long have she and her husband lived in England? OR How long have she and her husband been living in England?

5

It's the second week of the fall semester.
I've ~~taken~~ *been taking* a business course with Professor McCarthy.
For the past two weeks, we've *been* studying people
who have ~~been becoming~~ *become* very successful in the world of business. As part of the course, we've been reading books by or about internationally famous businesspeople.

For example, I've just ~~been finishing~~ *finished* a book by Bill Gates, the CEO of Microsoft, called *Business @ the Speed of Thought*. It was fascinating. Since then, I've ~~read~~ *been reading* *Business as Unusual* by Anita Roddick, the owner of The Body Shop. I've only ~~been reading~~ *read* about 50 pages of the the book so far, but it seems interesting.
Although I ~~bought~~ *'ve been buying* OR *'ve bought* her products ever since one of her stores opened in my neighborhood, I really didn't know much about her.

UNIT 21 (pages 99–102)

1

Proper nouns: Chirac, December, Korean, Todd
Common count nouns: chair, class, country, cup, euro, garden, hamburger, month, pen, president, snowflake, story
Common non-count nouns: furniture, history, honesty, ink, money, news, oil, rice, snow, spaghetti, sugar, swimming, water

2

2. Potatoes are, Rice is
3. Potato chips are, Americans eat . . . people
4. kills
5. Popcorn is
6. Peanuts are not
7. Peanut butter has
8. history . . . is
9. Ice cream is, Vanilla and chocolate are

3

2. many (c)   6. many (b)
3. much (b)   7. much (b)
4. many (c)   8. many (a)
5. much (b)

4

1. b. many
   c. a few
2. a. a lot of
   b. some
   c. a little
   d. enough
3. a. many
   b. any
   c. several
   d. a lot of
4. a. enough
   b. little

5

Answers will vary.

UNIT 22 (pages 103–106)

1

1. the . . . the
2. the
3. the
4. the, the
5. a, The . . . the
6. the
7. Ø, Ø, the . . . Ø
8. the, a
9. an, a
10. Ø, Ø
11. some, a . . . the . . . the
12. the, a, The

2

2. a	**13.** The
3. the	**14.** the
4. A	**15.** the
5. a	**16.** the
6. —	**17.** the
7. —	**18.** the
8. a	**19.** an
9. —	**20.** —
10. The	**21.** a
11. —	**22.** —
12. a	**23.** the

3

2. a	**15.** an
3. a	**16.** the
4. the	**17.** the
5. the	**18.** The
6. the	**19.** a
7. the	**20.** the
8. the	**21.** the
9. the	**22.** the
10. The	**23.** The
11. the	**24.** the
12. a	**25.** the
13. the	**26.** —
14. the	**27.** the

4

2. a	
3. the	
4. a	
5. a	
6. a	
7. —	
8. —	
9. the	
10. The	
11. a	
12. —	
13. —	
14. —	
15. —	
16. A OR The	
17. an	
18. a	
19. —	
20. a OR the	
21. —	
22. the	

UNIT 23 (pages 107–110)

1

2. nice	**11.** sudden
3. fast	**12.** carefully
4. well	**13.** angrily
5. dangerous	**14.** unfortunate
6. beautifully	**15.** badly
7. hard	**16.** thoughtful
8. safely	**17.** hungry
9. occasional	**18.** extremely
10. happy	

2

2. Good news travels fast!
3. It has five large rooms,
4. it's in a very large building,
5. it's very sunny.
6. It's not too bad.
7. It seems pretty quiet.
8. the landlord speaks very loudly.
9. He doesn't hear well.
10. Was it a hard decision?
11. we had to decide quickly.
12. I have to leave now.
13. Good luck with your new apartment!

3

2. hard	**15.** empty
3. well	**16.** good
4. nice	**17.** easily
5. extremely	**18.** near
6. comfortable	**19.** frequently
7. cold	**20.** nice
8. pretty	**21.** convenient
9. friendly	**22.** wonderful
10. safe	**23.** completely
11. really	**24.** new
12. important	**25.** really
13. late	**26.** happy
14. completely	**27.** happy

4

2. disturbed	**11.** touching
3. entertaining	**12.** astonishing
4. disgusted	**13.** frightening
5. inspiring	**14.** bored
6. paralyzed	**15.** disappointed
7. moving	**16.** touching
8. moved	**17.** exciting
9. frightening	**18.** entertaining
10. disturbed	**19.** bored

UNIT 24 (pages 111–116)

1

2. worse
3. bigger
4. more careful
5. cheaper
6. more comfortable
7. more dangerous
8. more difficult
9. earlier
10. more expensive
11. farther OR further
12. better
13. hotter
14. longer
15. noisier
16. prettier
17. slower
18. more terrible
19. wetter
20. wider

2

2. not as large as
3. just as big as
4. just as expensive as
5. not as varied as
6. not as long as
7. not as convenient as
8. not as late as
9. not as nice as
10. just as good as
11. not as good as
12. just as clean as

3

2. earlier
3. more comfortable
4. healthier than
5. better than
6. more exciting
7. taller than
8. quieter (OR more quiet) than
9. worse
10. later than
11. faster
12. easier

4

2. Y . . . cheaper than . . . X
3. Y . . . larger than . . . X
4. X . . . smaller than . . . Y
5. Y . . . heavier than . . . X
6. X . . . lighter than . . . Y
7. X . . . more efficient than . . . Y
8. Y . . . more effective than . . . X
9. Y . . . faster than . . . X
10. X . . . slower than . . . Y
11. X . . . noisier than . . . Y
12. Y . . . quieter (OR more quiet) than . . . X
13. Y . . . better than . . . X
14. X . . . worse than . . . Y

5

2. cheaper and cheaper OR less and less expensive
3. better and better
4. bigger and bigger
5. more and more varied
6. more and more popular
7. less and less healthy
8. heavier and heavier

6

2. The fresher the ingredients, the better the food.
3. The more popular the restaurant, the longer the lines.
4. The more enjoyable the meal, the more satisfied the customers.
5. The bigger the selection, the happier the customers.
6. The later in the day, the more tired the servers.
7. The more crowded the restaurant, the slower the service.
8. The better the service, the higher the tip.

7

Answers will vary.

UNIT 25 (pages 117–121)

1

2. the worst
3. the biggest
4. the cutest
5. the most dangerous
6. the most expensive
7. the farthest OR the furthest
8. the funniest
9. the best
10. the happiest OR the most happy
11. the hottest
12. the most important
13. the most intelligent
14. the most interesting
15. the lowest
16. the nicest
17. the noisiest
18. the most practical
19. the warmest
20. the most wonderful

2

2. Mexico City . . . the newest
3. New York City . . . the longest
4. Toronto . . . the shortest
5. The busiest . . . Mexico City
6. Toronto . . . the lowest
7. Toronto . . . the most expensive (OR Mexico City . . . the least expensive)
8. the cheapest . . . Mexico City

3

2. the least comfortable
3. the newest
4. the most beautiful
5. the easiest
6. the biggest
7. the fastest
8. the coolest
9. the hottest
10. the most convenient

11. the most interesting
12. the least dangerous
13. the most historic
14. the most crowded
15. The most efficient
16. the most dangerous
17. the least expensive
18. the quietest OR the most quiet

4

Greetings from Mexico City! With its mixture of the old and the new, this is one of the
~~interestingest~~ *most interesting* cities I've ever visited. The people are among the ~~friendlier~~ *friendliest* OR *most friendly* in the world, and they have been very patient with my attempts to speak their language. Spanish is definitely one of ~~a~~ *the* most beautiful languages, and I definitely want to take lessons when I get home. This has been the ~~most hot~~ *hottest* summer in years, and I'm looking forward to going to the beach next week. The air pollution is also the ~~baddest~~ *worst* I've experienced, so I'll be glad to be out of the city. By the way, we definitely did not need to rent a car. The ~~most fast~~ *fastest* and ~~convenientest~~ *most convenient* way to get around is by subway.

5

Answers will vary.

UNIT 26 (pages 122–126)

1

2. more beautifully	the most beautifully
3. more carefully	the most carefully
4. more dangerously	the most dangerously
5. earlier	the earliest
6. farther OR further	the farthest OR the furthest
7. faster	the fastest
8. more quickly	the most quickly
9. sooner	the soonest
10. better	the best

2

2. ran as fast as
3. jumped as high as
4. didn't jump as high as
5. didn't throw the discus as far as
6. threw the discus as far as
7. didn't do as well as
8. didn't compete as successfully as

3

2. harder than
3. more slowly than OR slower than
4. faster
5. more accurately
6. more aggressively than
7. worse than
8. better
9. more successfully
10. more seriously
11. (more) regularly

Winning Team: George, Bob, Randy, Dennis
Losing Team: Alex, Rick, Larry, Elvin

4

2. E . . . the most slowly OR the slowest, more slowly OR slower than
3. higher than . . . B
4. E . . . the highest
5. farther than . . . E
6. E . . . the farthest
7. E . . . the best
8. E . . . the worst . . . better than

5

2. She's running more and more frequently.
3. He's throwing the ball farther and farther.
4. She's shooting more and more accurately.
5. He's jumping higher and higher.
6. He's running more and more slowly OR slower and slower.
7. They're skating more and more gracefully. OR They're scoring higher and higher.
8. They're practicing harder and harder.
9. He's driving more and more dangerously.
10. They're feeling worse and worse.

6

I just completed my run. I'm running much longer ~~that~~ *than* before.

Today I ran for 30 minutes without getting out of breath. I'm glad I decided to run ~~more slow~~ *more slowly* OR *slower*. The more slowly I run, the ~~farthest~~ *farther* I can go. I'm really seeing progress.

Because I'm enjoying it, I run more and more ~~frequent~~ *frequently*. And the more often I do it, the longer and farther I can go. I really believe that running helps me feel better more ~~quick~~ *quickly* than other forms of exercise. I'm even sleeping better than before!

I'm thinking about running in the next marathon. I may not run ~~as fast than~~ *as fast as* OR *faster than* younger

runners, but I think I can run ~~long~~ *longer* and farther.
We'll see!

UNIT 27 (pages 127–130)

1

2. going	7. doing
3. meeting	8. taking
4. Sitting	9. Exercising
5. running	10. wasting
6. lifting	

2

2. Dancing
3. lifting weights
4. walking (OR playing tennis) . . . playing tennis (OR walking)
5. swimming
6. lifting weights
7. walking (OR riding a bike) . . . riding a bike (OR walking)
8. Doing sit-ups
9. swimming
10. lifting weights (OR doing sit-ups), doing sit-ups (OR lifting weights)
11. running
12. playing tennis
13. Riding a bike
14. lifting weights

3

2. dislikes doing OR doesn't enjoy doing
3. enjoys dancing
4. mind teaching
5. kept practicing
6. denied (OR denies) stepping OR didn't admit (OR doesn't admit) stepping
7. considering taking
8. regrets not beginning
9. suggests going
10. admits feeling

4

Answers will vary.

UNIT 28 (pages 131–134)

1

2. of	7. in
3. to	8. on
4. of	9. to
5. to	10. in
6. about	

2

2. succeeded in collecting
3. is worried about missing
4. are used to working
5. believe in talking
6. are tired of waiting
7. insists on reaching
8. approves of having
9. are opposed to going
10. looking forward to returning

3

2. striking	7. missing
3. firing	8. trying
4. permitting	9. making
5. being	10. listening
6. getting	11. seeing

4

Answers will vary.

UNIT 29 (pages 135–138)

1

2. want to see
3. refuses to go
4. threatened to end
5. hesitate (OR am hesitating) to take
6. seems to be
7. attempted to create
8. intend to stay
9. needs to speak
10. will agree to go

2

2. to do the dishes.
   him to do the dishes.
3. her to buy some milk.
   to buy some milk.
4. him to drive her to her aunt's.
   to drive her to her aunt's.
5. him to have dinner at her place Friday night.
   to have dinner at her place Friday night.
6. him to give her his answer tomorrow.
   to give her his answer tomorrow.
7. to cut his hair.
   her to cut his hair.
8. him to be home at 7:00.
   to get home at 8:00.
9. her to call him before she leaves the office.
   to call him before she left the office.
10. to see a movie Friday night.
    her to pick one out.

3

Annie answered my letter! She advised ~~we~~ *us* to go to counseling separately. I don't know if John will agree ~~going~~ *to go*, but I'm going to ask him to think about it. I attempted to introduce the topic last night, but he pretended ~~to not~~ *not to* hear me. I won't give up, though. I'm going to try to persuade ~~he~~ *him* to go. If he agrees to go, I may ask Annie ^*to* recommend some counselors in our area. I want ~~finding~~ *to find* someone really good. Our relationship deserves to have a chance, and I'm prepared ^*to* give it one. But I want John ~~feels~~ *to feel* the same way. I need to know that he's 100% committed to the relationship. I can be patient, but I can't afford ~~waiting~~ *to wait* forever.

4

Answers will vary.

UNIT 30 (pages 139–141)

1

3. He uses most of his salary (in order) to pay his college tuition.
4. He really wants an MP3 player (in order) to download music from the Internet.
5. He's going to wait for a sale in order not to pay the full price.
6. A lot of people came into the store today (in order) to look at the new gadgets.
7. They like talking to Ned (in order) to get information about the gadgets.
8. Someone bought an electronic navigator in order not to get lost.
9. Another person bought a tiny camcorder (in order) to bring it on vacation.
10. She used her credit card in order not to pay right away.
11. Ned showed her how to use the camcorder (in order) to do a lot of things.
12. She'll use it as a camera (in order) to take videos.

2

2. (in order) to return
3. in order not to pay
4. (in order) to carry
5. (in order) to sign
6. to have
7. (in order) to cut
8. (in order) to find out
9. in order not to miss
10. in order not to waste

3

I went to the store ~~for~~ *to* get some eggs and other things for dinner. I set the alarm on the electronic organizer to remind you to put the turkey in the oven. Could you call Cindi ~~too~~ *to* ask her to bring some dessert? Tell her she should come straight from school in order ~~to be not~~ *not to be* late. We'll eat at 6:00—if that's OK with you. Remember— you can use the organizer ~~for checking~~ *to check* the vegetable casserole recipe. I've got to run in order to get back in time to help you! Could I use your new camcorder ^*in* order to film the event?

UNIT 31 (pages 142–145)

1

2. The story is too long to fit on one page.
3. Ed Smith was nice enough to give us an interview.
4. These computers are getting too old for us to use.
5. The bookshelves aren't low enough for me to reach.
6. This newspaper has gotten good enough to win an award.
7. It's too noisy for me to concentrate.
8. The students are too busy to take a break.
9. Tina is good enough to work on a major newspaper.

Positive points: 3, 6, 9
Negative points: 2, 4, 5, 7, 8

2

2. late enough to call
3. too heavy for me to lift
4. too sweet to drink
5. small enough to fit
6. too noisy for me to think
7. too young to graduate
8. not hot enough to need
9. not sick enough to call
10. too high for me to reach
11. too tired to stay
12. good enough to go

3

I really think that people under 21 are too young ~~for driving~~ *to drive*. They are just not ~~enough~~ ~~experienced~~ *experienced* *enough* to operate a car. Driving is a risky activity, and the consequences are too important to ignore.

I totally agree that 13 is ~~to~~ *too* young to drive, but 21—come on, now! In my opinion, a 16-year-old is responsible enough ~~getting~~ *to get* behind the wheel of a car.

Everyone is talking about a MINIMUM age for driving. Well, what about a MAXIMUM? I think people over 75 are too old ~~too~~ *to* drive. Their physical reactions are just not ~~enough quick~~ *quick enough* anymore to drive.

Why don't they just require older people to take a road test every few years? The law requires us to test our <u>cars</u> every year. If it's important enough to check the car, it should be important enough ~~be~~ to check the driver! If you're good enough to pass the test, then you're good enough *to* ^ drive. Period!

I don't think it's a question of too young or too old to drive. Younger people have a quicker reaction time, but older people have more experience. The important question is this: Is the person competent enough ~~being~~ *to be* on the road? Age alone just isn't that important.

4

Answers will vary.

UNIT 32 (pages 146–149)

1

2. living	**8.** to do
3. Flying	**9.** to live
4. to get	**10.** to do
5. flying	**11.** seeing
6. to get over	**12.** to visit
7. doing	**13.** getting

2

2. is tired of being	**7.** stopped to get
3. quit (OR stopped) drinking	**8.** afford to lose
4. believes in talking	**9.** refuses to live
5. forgot to bring	**10.** intends to make
6. remember telling	**11.** agreed to help
	12. offered to drive

3

3. It's useful to work together.
4. Being careful is smart.
5. Being afraid all the time isn't good.
6. It isn't dangerous to fly.
7. It's a good idea to do relaxation exercises.
8. It's wonderful to travel.

4

Answers will vary.

UNIT 33 (pages 150–153)

1

2. listen to music than surf the net.
3. reading a book to hanging out with friends.
4. hanging out with friends to talking on the phone.
5. go to the movies than watch TV.
6. talk on the phone than listen to music.
7. going to the movies to playing computer games.
8. watching TV to listening to music.
9. read a book than watch TV.
10. reading a book to playing computer games.

2

2. He'd prefer (to have OR having) juice.
3. He'd rather have tomato juice than apple juice.
4. He'd rather not have a hot beverage.
5. He'd prefer not to have chicken soup.
6. He'd prefer a sandwich to cottage cheese and fruit.
7. He'd prefer a turkey sandwich to a tuna fish sandwich.
8. He'd rather have white bread.
9. He'd rather not have chocolate pudding.
10. He'd prefer vanilla ice cream to chocolate ice cream.

3

2. Do you prefer	**6.** Would (OR Do) you prefer
3. Would you prefer	
4. would you rather	**7.** Would (OR Do) you prefer
5. Would (OR Do) you prefer	
	8. Do you prefer

4

Answers will vary.

UNIT 34 (pages 154–158)

1

2. must pass	**9.** must not leave
3. must not forget	**10.** must wear
4. must obey	**11.** must not talk
5. must stop	**12.** must sit
6. must not drive	**13.** must . . . drink
7. must not change	**14.** must know
8. must turn on	

2

2. don't have to be
3. have to drive
4. doesn't have to drive
5. have to drive
6. don't have to wear
7. have to wear
8. have to have
9. don't have to have
10. have to keep
11. don't have to keep
12. have to wear

3

2. don't have to
3. don't have to
4. must not
5. don't have to
6. doesn't have to
7. must not
8. don't have to
9. don't have to
10. must not

4

2. A: Do . . . have to stop
   B: Yes, we do.
3. A: have . . . had to use
4. A: Did . . . have to work
   B: No, I didn't.
5. B: 'll have to get OR 'm going to have to get
6. B: had to drive
7. B: did . . . have to pay
8. A: Has . . . had to pay
   B: No, he hasn't.
9. A: Will (OR Do) . . . have to get
   OR Are . . . going to have to get
   B: Yes, I will. OR I do. OR I am.
10. B: has to have

5

2. b
3. b
4. c
5. a
6. b
7. a
8. b

6

Answers will vary.

UNIT 35 (pages 159–162)

1

2. is supposed to send
3. are supposed to provide
4. aren't supposed to provide
5. isn't supposed to pay for
6. is supposed to pay for
7. aren't supposed to pay for
8. is supposed to pay for
9. aren't supposed to give
10. are supposed to give
11. isn't supposed to supply
12. is supposed to pay for

2

2. Item 2. She was supposed to write the month first. OR She wasn't supposed to write the day first.
3. Item 4. She was supposed to print (OR write) her last name. OR She wasn't supposed to print (OR write) her first name.
4. Item 5. She was supposed to print (OR write) her first name. OR She wasn't supposed to print (OR write) her last name.
5. Item 6. She was supposed to write (OR include) her zip code.
6. Item 7. She was supposed to write (OR include) her state and (her) zip code.
7. Item 8. She was supposed to sign her name. OR She wasn't supposed to print her name.
8. Item 9. She was supposed to write the date.

3

1. is (OR was) supposed to land
2. are . . . supposed to get
3. Are . . . supposed to call
   Yes, we are.
4. are . . . supposed to tip
5. Is . . . supposed to be
   No, it isn't.
6. are . . . supposed to do
   're supposed to leave
7. Is . . . supposed to rain
   No, it isn't.
8. Are . . . supposed to shake

4

2. a. Adam wasn't going to get married.
   b. He was going to stay single.
3. a. Erica and Adam were going to get married in June.
   b. They weren't going to get married in September.
4. a. They weren't going to have a big wedding.
   b. They were going to have a small one.
5. a. They were going to live in Boston.
   b. They weren't going to move to Amherst.
6. a. Adam wasn't going to change jobs.
   b. He was going to keep his old one.

5

Answers will vary.

UNIT 36 (pages 163–166)

1

2. may go
3. could be
4. might be able to
5. might want
6. may not be
7. could go
8. might not understand
9. might not want
10. could stay
11. might be

2

2. might buy
3. is going to rain
4. is going to see
5. might go
6. is going to work
7. might have
8. is going to call
9. is going to read
10. might write

3

How are you? It's the Fourth of July, and it's raining really hard. They say it could clear up later. Then again, it ~~could~~ *might OR may* not. You never know with the weather.

Do you remember my brother, Eric? He says hi. He might ~~has~~ *have* dinner with me on Saturday night. We may go to a new Mexican restaurant that just opened in the mall.

I definitely ~~might take~~ *am going to take OR am taking* some vacation time next month. Perhaps we could do something together. It might ~~not~~ be fun to do some traveling. What do you think? Let me know.

4

Answers will vary.

UNIT 37 (pages 167–172)

1

2. must not be
3. must feel
4. must not have
5. must know
6. must have
7. must not hear
8. must feel
9. must speak
10. must not study
11. must have
12. must not eat

2

1. might
2. must
3. must
4. might, could
5. could, must
6. must, couldn't

3

2. She must
3. They must
4. He must be
5. She might OR may OR could
6. It must be
7. They might be OR may be OR could be
8. She must
9. He might be OR may be OR could be
10. They must be

4

2. Could
3. can't
4. Bob
5. Chet
6. could
7. might
8. Dave
9. could
10. couldn't
11. Allen

5

Answers will vary.

6

Just got home. It's really cold outside. The temperature ~~could~~ *must* be below freezing because the walkway is all covered with ice. What a day! We went down to the police station to look at photos. They must ~~having~~ *have* hundreds of photos. They kept showing us more and more. We kept looking, but it was difficult to be sure. After all, we only saw the burglar for a few seconds. They've ~~gotta~~ *got to* have other witnesses besides us! There were a lot of people at the mall that day. We ~~may not~~ *can't OR couldn't* be the only ones who got a look at the burglar! That's the one thing I'm certain of! In spite of our uncertainty with the photos, the detective was very patient. I guess he must be used to witnesses like us. Nevertheless, it ~~have~~ *has* to be frustrating for him. I know the police ~~may~~ *must* really want to catch this guy.

Test: Units 1–8

PART ONE

Circle the letter of the correct answer to complete each sentence.

Example
Jason never _____ coffee.

(A) drink   (C) is drinking
(B) drinks   (D) was drinking

A (B) C D

1. At the moment, Meng _____ on a report.

(A) doesn't work   (C) work
(B) is working   (D) works

A B C D

2. Water _____ at 100° C.

(A) boil   (C) boils
(B) boiling   (D) is boiling

A B C D

3. What _____ these days?

(A) are you doing   (C) you are doing
(B) do you do   (D) you do

A B C D

4. Do you have any aspirin? Ryan _____ a headache.

(A) are having   (C) have
(B) has   (D) is having

A B C D

5. Maria _____ to the park every day.

(A) does   (C) goes
(B) go   (D) is going

A B C D

6. When you get to the corner, _____ left.

(A) is turning   (C) turning
(B) turn   (D) turns

A B C D

7. Walk! _____ run!

(A) Don't   (C) Not
(B) No   (D) You don't

A B C D

8. Jennifer never _____ in the ocean.

(A) is swimming   (C) swimming
(B) swim   (D) swims

A B C D

(continued)

9. —Do you like spaghetti?
    —Yes, I _____.
    A B C D

    (A) am   **(C)** don't
    (B) do   **(D)** like

10. Tyler _____ me at 9:00 last night.
    A B C D

    (A) called   **(C)** is calling
    (B) calls   **(D)** was calling

11. There _____ a lot of people in the park yesterday.
    A B C D

    (A) are   **(C)** was
    (B) is   **(D)** were

12. One day last March, I _____ a very strange letter.
    A B C D

    (A) did get   **(C)** used to get
    (B) got   **(D)** was getting

13. Where _____ to school?
    A B C D

    (A) did you go   **(C)** you go
    (B) you did go   **(D)** you went

14. Claude didn't _____ in Canada.
    A B C D

    (A) lived   **(C)** used to live
    (B) use to live   **(D)** used to living

15. Lauren left class early because she _____ a terrible headache.
    A B C D

    (A) had   **(C)** used to have
    (B) have   **(D)** was having

16. _____ is your English teacher?
    A B C D

    (A) Who   **(C)** Whose
    (B) Whom   **(D)** Why

17. Who _____ yesterday at the store?
    A B C D

    (A) did you see   **(C)** you saw
    (B) did you use to see   **(D)** you were seeing

18. As soon as the light turned red, she _____ the car.
    A B C D

    (A) did stop   **(C)** stops
    (B) stopped   **(D)** was stopping

19. They _____ when the phone rang.
    A B C D

    (A) sleep   **(C)** was sleeping
    (B) slept   **(D)** were sleeping

20. Josh _____ the paper when I interrupted him.   **A B C D**

    (**A**) read   (**C**) was reading
    (**B**) reads   (**D**) were reading

21. —Who _____ there?   **A B C D**
    —Mr. Jackson saw me.

    (**A**) did you see   (**C**) you saw
    (**B**) saw you   (**D**) you see

22. —Whose teacher _____?   **A B C D**
    —I called Kayla's teacher.

    (**A**) called you   (**C**) you called
    (**B**) did you call   (**D**) were calling

23. It _____ tomorrow.   **A B C D**

    (**A**) rains   (**C**) 's going to rain
    (**B**) rained   (**D**) 's raining

24. Don't eat so much. You _____ sick later.   **A B C D**

    (**A**) 're feeling   (**C**) felt
    (**B**) feel   (**D**) 'll feel

25. The package will _____ tomorrow.   **A B C D**

    (**A**) arrive   (**C**) arriving
    (**B**) arrives   (**D**) be going to arrive

26. What _____ you do next month when you finish this course?   **A B C D**

    (**A**) are   (**C**) do
    (**B**) did   (**D**) will

27. Good night. I _____ tomorrow.   **A B C D**

    (**A**) 'll see you   (**C**) 'm seeing you
    (**B**) 'm going to see you   (**D**) see

28. Miguel and I _____ to the Crash concert. We already have our tickets.   **A B C D**

    (**A**) are going   (**C**) went
    (**B**) go   (**D**) will go

29. What will Michiko do when she _____ her license?   **A B C D**

    (**A**) gets   (**C**) is going to get
    (**B**) is getting   (**D**) will get

30. That driver _____ a speeding ticket. The police are right behind him.   **A B C D**

    (**A**) gets   (**C**) is going to get
    (**B**) is getting   (**D**) will get

(continued)

31. In the future, more cars _____ on electricity.　　　　　　　A B C D

    (A) are running　　　　(C) run
    (B) ran　　　　　　　　(D) will run

32. According to this schedule, the next train _____ in 10 minutes.　A B C D

    (A) leave　　　　　　　(C) left
    (B) leaves　　　　　　(D) leaving

33. —Will you be home tomorrow night?　　　　　　　　　　　A B C D
    —No, _____.

    (A) I don't　　　　　　(C) I will
    (B) I'm not　　　　　　(D) I won't

34. I'll see you _____.　　　　　　　　　　　　　　　　A B C D

    (A) at the moment　　　(C) last night
    (B) in an hour　　　　　(D) usually

35. —Why did you borrow those chairs from Andy?　　　　　　A B C D
    —I _____ a party next Saturday night.

    (A) had　　　　　　　　(C) 'm going to have
    (B) have　　　　　　　(D) 'll have

36. —Call me when you get home.　　　　　　　　　　　　A B C D
    —Don't worry. I _____.

    (A) don't forget　　　　(C) 'm not forgetting
    (B) forget　　　　　　(D) won't forget

PART TWO

Each sentence has four underlined words or phrases. The four underlined parts of the sentence are marked A, B, C, and D. Circle the letter of the <u>one</u> underlined word or phrase that is NOT CORRECT.

    Example
    Ana <u>rarely</u> <u>is drinking</u> coffee, but <u>this morning</u> she <u>is having</u> a cup.　A Ⓑ C D
        A　　　B　　　　　　　　　C　　　　　　D

37. Nicole <u>usually</u> <u>drives</u> to work, but <u>today</u> she <u>takes</u> the train.　A B C D
        A　　　B　　　　　　　　C　　　D

38. Carlos <u>usually</u> doesn't <u>eat</u> pizza, but <u>at</u> the moment he <u>is wanting</u> a slice.　A B C D
       A　　　　　　B　　　　　C　　　　　　D

39. Frank <u>rarely</u> <u>goes</u> downtown because he <u>doesn't</u> <u>likes</u> the crowded streets.　A B C D
       A　　　B　　　　　　　　　　C　　　D

40. Emily <u>usually</u> <u>is eating</u> in the cafeteria, but <u>these days</u> she <u>is eating</u> in the park.　A B C D
       A　　　B　　　　　　　　　　　C　　　　　D

41. <u>What</u> <u>you are</u> <u>studying</u> these days <u>at school</u>?　A B C D
    A　　B　　　C　　　　　　D

42. Rachel <u>don't</u> <u>speak</u> French, but <u>she's</u> <u>studying</u> Spanish at the Adult Center.　A B C D
       A　　B　　　　　　C　　D

43. John <u>loves</u> tennis, but <u>rarely he</u> <u>plays</u> because he <u>doesn't have</u> time.　A B C D
    A　　　　　　　B　　C　　　　　　D

44. <u>Stand</u> up straight, <u>breathe</u> deeply, <u>hold</u> your head up, and <u>no look</u> down.
     A   B   C   D   A B C D

45. Megan <u>works always</u> late and <u>is rarely</u> home before 8:00 <u>at night</u>.
              A   B C   D   A B C D

46. I <u>know</u> you usually <u>don't wear</u> a jacket, but <u>wear</u> one today because it   A B C D
      A   B   C
<u>is feeling</u> cold outside.
    D

47. A breeze <u>is blowing</u>, the <u>sun</u> <u>shines</u>, and the sky <u>looks</u> clear and bright.
                 A   B C   D   A B C D

48. Paulo <u>was</u> <u>drying</u> the dishes <u>when</u> he <u>was dropping</u> the plate.
          A   B   C   D   A B C D

49. When Anna <u>were</u> a little girl, she <u>used to pretend</u> that she <u>had</u> a horse.
          A   B   C   D   A B C D

50. What <u>did</u> you <u>used to do</u> when you <u>felt</u> afraid?
        A   B C   D   A B C D

51. <u>As soon as</u> the alarm clock <u>rang</u>, she <u>woke up</u> and <u>was getting</u> out of bed.
      A   B   C   D   A B C D

52. Once <u>when</u> I <u>was</u> a little boy, I <u>used to get</u> sick and <u>went</u> to the hospital.
        A   B   C   D   A B C D

53. Who <u>you did</u> <u>see</u> when you <u>left</u> the building <u>last night</u>?
        A   B   C   D   A B C D

54. <u>While</u> I <u>drove</u> home, I <u>turned on</u> the radio and <u>heard</u> the news about   A B C D
     A   B   C   D
the accident.

55. When Marie <u>will get</u> <u>home</u>, she <u>is going to</u> <u>call</u> me.
            A   B   C   D   A B C D

56. <u>As soon as</u> she <u>finds</u> a new <u>job</u>, she <u>tells</u> her boss.
      A   B   C   D   A B C D

57. <u>I'll make</u> some sandwiches <u>before</u> <u>I'll leave</u> for the office <u>in the morning</u>.
      A   B   C   D   A B C D

58. According to the weather <u>forecast</u>, it <u>going to be</u> hot and sunny <u>tomorrow</u>   A B C D
                       A   B   C
with a chance of a thunderstorm <u>in the afternoon</u>.
                          D

59. The doors <u>will</u> open until the train <u>comes</u> to a <u>complete</u> <u>stop</u>.
         A   B   C   D   A B C D

60. My sister <u>is going to be</u> 16 <u>next</u> month, and she <u>has</u> a big party with all her A B C D
          A   B   C   D
friends.

Test: Units 9–10

PART ONE

Circle the letter of the correct answer to complete each sentence.

Example
Jason never _____ coffee.

(**A**) drink   (**C**) is drinking
(**B**) drinks   (**D**) was drinking

A Ⓑ C D

1. Kayla lives by _____, but she's looking for a roommate.

(**A**) her   (**C**) himself
(**B**) herself   (**D**) ourselves

A B C D

2. People in my office exchange cards with _____ during the holidays.

(**A**) myself   (**C**) ourselves
(**B**) one another   (**D**) themselves

A B C D

3. Thanks for offering to help, but I think I can do it _____.

(**A**) herself   (**C**) itself
(**B**) himself   (**D**) myself

A B C D

4. —Sara is talking to Austin.
   —I didn't know that they knew _____.

(**A**) each other   (**C**) them
(**B**) others   (**D**) themselves

A B C D

5. —Did you say something to me?
   —No, I'm just talking to _____. I do that sometimes when I'm cooking.

(**A**) me   (**C**) oneself
(**B**) myself   (**D**) you

A B C D

6. —There's soda in the refrigerator. Help _____.
   —Thanks.

(**A**) me   (**C**) you
(**B**) myself   (**D**) yourself

A B C D

7. —Where are your books?
   —I put _____.

(**A**) away   (**C**) them away
(**B**) away them   (**D**) them off

A B C D

8. It's an interesting story. Please _____.　　　　　　　　　　A　B　C　D

   (**A**) carry out　　　　　　(**C**) hand in
   (**B**) go on　　　　　　　　(**D**) write up

9. When Mei-Ling doesn't know a word, she always looks it _____　　A　B　C　D
   in the dictionary.

   (**A**) at　　　　　　　　　(**C**) over
   (**B**) into　　　　　　　　(**D**) up

10. Please e-mail _____ when you get home.　　　　　　　　　A　B　C　D

   (**A**) me　　　　　　　　　(**C**) you
   (**B**) myself　　　　　　　(**D**) yourself

11. It's my own fault. That's why I'm angry at _____.　　　　　　A　B　C　D

   (**A**) him　　　　　　　　(**C**) me
   (**B**) himself　　　　　　(**D**) myself

PART TWO

Each sentence has four underlined words or phrases. The four underlined parts of the sentence are marked A, B, C, and D. Circle the letter of the <u>one</u> underlined word or phrase that is NOT CORRECT.

   Example
   Ana <u>rarely</u> <u>is drinking</u> coffee, but <u>this morning</u> she <u>is having</u> a cup.　A Ⓑ C D
         A   B   C   D

12. Could we talk <u>over it</u> before you <u>turn</u> the whole <u>idea</u> <u>down</u>?　　　A　B　C　D
            A   B   C D

13. Ethan <u>stood</u> <u>up</u> and introduced <u>himself</u> to <u>myself</u>.　　　　　A　B　C　D
        A   B   C   D

14. Marta <u>herself</u> <u>call</u> the meeting <u>off</u> <u>yesterday</u>.　　　　　　A　B　C　D
         A   B   C D

15. Do you want to get up <u>by yourself</u>, or would you like me to <u>wake up you</u>?　A　B　C　D
                 A   B   C   D

16. Don't <u>clean</u> <u>up</u> the kitchen by <u>itself</u>; I'd be glad to <u>help out</u>.　　A　B　C　D
       A   B   C   D

17. Rachel and Kevin know <u>themselves</u> well because <u>they</u> <u>grew</u> <u>up</u> together.　A　B　C　D
                  A   B C D

18. Antonio and Monica always <u>look over</u> <u>each other</u> homework before they　A　B　C　D
                    A   B

   <u>hand</u> <u>it in</u>.
   C   D

19. Before they <u>turned</u> <u>the music</u> <u>down</u>, I couldn't hear <u>me</u> think!　　A　B　C　D
          A   B   C   D

20. Tom asked <u>me</u> to <u>pick</u> some stamps for <u>him</u> at the post office <u>up</u>.　　A　B　C　D
          A   B   C   D

Test: Units 11–15

PART ONE

Circle the letter of the correct answer to complete each sentence.

Example
Jason never _____ coffee.   A Ⓑ C D

(A) drink   (C) is drinking
(B) drinks   (D) was drinking

1. —Would you shut the door, please?   A B C D
   —_____

   (A) Certainly.   (C) Yes, I could.
   (B) No, I can't.   (D) Yes, I would.

2. Why _____ a movie tonight?   A B C D

   (A) about seeing   (C) not seeing
   (B) don't we see   (D) we don't see

3. Courtney can't speak German yet, but after a few lessons she _____   A B C D
   speak a little.

   (A) can   (C) is able to
   (B) could   (D) will be able to

4. In 2002, Canadian figure skaters Jamie Salé and David Pelletier _____   A B C D
   win the gold medal at the Winter Olympics.

   (A) can   (C) was able to
   (B) could   (D) were able to

5. I _____ make new friends since I moved here.   A B C D

   (A) can't   (C) haven't been able to
   (B) couldn't   (D) 'm not able to

6. She _____ better not arrive late.   A B C D

   (A) did   (C) had
   (B) has   (D) would

7. —Do you mind if I borrow a chair?   A B C D
   —_____ Do you need only one?

   (A) I'm sorry.   (C) Yes, I do.
   (B) Not at all.   (D) Yes, I would.

8. Would you mind _____ me tomorrow?　　　　　　　　　　　A B C D

    (A) call　　　　　　　　　　**(C)** to call
    (B) calling　　　　　　　　**(D)** if you call

9. You _____ miss the deadline or you'll have to pay a late fee.　　A B C D

    (A) better not　　　　　　　**(C)** 'd better not
    (B) 'd better　　　　　　　　**(D)** had no better

10. _____ take the train instead of the bus? It's faster.　　　　A B C D

    (A) How about　　　　　　　**(C)** Why don't
    (B) Let's　　　　　　　　　　**(D)** Why not

11. May my sister _____ to class with me tomorrow?　　　　　A B C D

    (A) come　　　　　　　　　　**(C)** coming
    (B) comes　　　　　　　　　**(D)** to come

12. A: Would you please explain that again?　　　　　　　　　A B C D
    B: Yes, _____.

    (A) certainly　　　　　　　　**(C)** not at all
    (B) I would　　　　　　　　　**(D)** I do

PART TWO

Each sentence has four underlined words or phrases. The four underlined parts of the sentence are marked A, B, C, and D. Circle the letter of the <u>one</u> underlined word or phrase that is NOT CORRECT.

Example
Ana <u>rarely</u> <u>is drinking</u> coffee, but <u>this morning</u> she <u>is having</u> a cup.　A Ⓑ C D
    A　　　**B**　　　　　　　　**C**　　　　　　**D**

13. When <u>you will</u> <u>be</u> <u>able</u> to <u>tell</u> me your decision?　　　　　A B C D
    A　　　**B**　　**C**　　**D**

14. <u>Why don't</u> <u>we</u> <u>see</u> a movie Friday <u>night.</u>　　　　　　　A B C D
    A　　　**B**　　**C**　　　　　　　**D**

15. <u>Do</u> you <u>mind</u> <u>when</u> I postpone our Wednesday <u>appointment?</u>　A B C D
    A　　　**B**　　**C**　　　　　　　　　　　**D**

16. <u>May</u> <u>he</u> <u>has</u> until <u>tomorrow</u> to hand in his paper?　　　　A B C D
    A　**B**　**C**　　　**D**

17. <u>Let's</u> <u>to leave</u> the party <u>early enough</u> <u>to catch</u> the last bus.　A B C D
    A　　**B**　　　　　　　**C**　　　**D**

18. <u>Could</u> you <u>remember</u> <u>to bring</u> home <u>please</u> the newspaper?　A B C D
    A　　　**B**　　　　**C**　　　　**D**

19. You really ought <u>be</u> <u>more</u> <u>careful</u> or you <u>'ll get</u> into trouble.　A B C D
    A　**B**　**C**　　　　**D**

20. <u>Would</u> you mind <u>to tell</u> me when you <u>are going to</u> <u>be</u> late?　A B C D
    A　　　　　　**B**　　　　　　　**C**　　　**D**

Test: Units 16–20

PART ONE

Circle the letter of the correct answer to complete each sentence.

Example
Jason never _____ coffee.   A (B) C D

(A) drink   (C) is drinking
(B) drinks   (D) was drinking

1. Samantha _____ in Mexico since 1991.   A B C D

   (A) is living   (C) have lived
   (B) has lived   (D) lived

2. John has already _____ this course.   A B C D

   (A) been taking   (C) takes
   (B) taken   (D) took

3. The journalist hasn't finished the article _____.   A B C D

   (A) already   (C) then
   (B) now   (D) yet

4. The department store has been in business _____ many years.   A B C D

   (A) already   (C) in
   (B) for   (D) since

5. How many cups of coffee have you _____ this morning?   A B C D

   (A) been drinking   (C) drink
   (B) drank   (D) drunk

6. Amanda _____ Texas six years ago.   A B C D

   (A) has been leaving   (C) left
   (B) has left   (D) used to leave

7. They have been _____ lunch in the same cafeteria for 10 years. A B C D

   (A) ate   (C) eaten
   (B) eat   (D) eating

8. The Jordans _____ at R & J Corporation since 1999.   A B C D

   (A) are working   (C) have been working
   (B) has been working   (D) worked

9. Have you read any good books _____?   A B C D

   (A) already   (C) lately
   (B) ever   (D) now

10. It _____ all day, so we haven't left the house.   A B C D

    (A) is raining   (C) rains
    (B) has been raining   (D) rained

11. —Has the mail come yet?   A B C D
    —Yes, it _____.

    (A) did   (C) have
    (B) has   (D) is

12. I'm sorry I'm late. How long _____?   A B C D

    (A) did you wait   (C) have you waited
    (B) have you been waiting (D) you have been waiting

13. —What are you doing?   A B C D
    —I _____ on this report all morning.

    (A) work   (C) 've worked
    (B) 've been working (D) worked

14. _____ you cut your hair lately?   A B C D

    (A) Are   (C) Were
    (B) Did   (D) Have

PART TWO

Each sentence has four underlined words or phrases. The four underlined parts of the sentence are marked A, B, C, and D. Circle the letter of the one underlined word or phrase that is NOT CORRECT.

Example
Ana <u>rarely</u> <u>is drinking</u> coffee, but <u>this morning</u> she <u>is having</u> a cup.   A Ⓑ C D
    A   B   C   D

15. <u>When</u> she <u>was</u> a child, she <u>has worked</u> in a factory <u>for</u> more than three years.   A B C D
    A   B   C   D

16. Eric <u>have</u> <u>been sleeping</u> <u>for</u> more than <u>three hours</u>.   A B C D
     A   B   C   D

17. Last night we <u>have rented</u> two <u>DVDs</u> and <u>watched</u> them with some <u>friends</u>.   A B C D
            A   B   C   D

18. Jennifer <u>hasn't done</u> a thing <u>since</u> she <u>has gotten</u> to work.   A B C D
        A   B   C   D

19. <u>Since</u> I <u>have known</u> Daniel, he <u>had</u> three different <u>jobs</u>.   A B C D
    A   B   C   D

20. She <u>hasn't</u> <u>washed</u> the dishes or <u>made</u> the beds <u>already</u>.   A B C D
    A   B   C   D

Test: Units 21–22

PART ONE

Circle the letter of the correct answer to complete each sentence. Choose Ø when no word is needed.

Example
Jason never _____ coffee.   A Ⓑ C D

(A) drink   (C) is drinking
(B) drinks   (D) was drinking

1. _____ the mail arrived yet?   A B C D

   (A) Are   (C) Has
   (B) Is   (D) Have

2. She was unhappy because _____ of her friends sent her a card.   A B C D

   (A) a few   (C) few
   (B) a little   (D) little

3. They didn't have _____ shoes in my size.   A B C D

   (A) a great deal of   (C) much
   (B) a lot of   (D) some

4. Can you lend me _____ money?   A B C D

   (A) little   (C) many
   (B) some   (D) a few

5. _____ university is larger than a college.   A B C D

   (A) A   (C) The
   (B) An   (D) Ø

6. That's _____ best story I've ever heard.   A B C D

   (A) a   (C) the
   (B) an   (D) Ø

7. Amber says that _____ music is her favorite free-time activity.   A B C D

   (A) a   (C) the
   (B) an   (D) Ø

8. You have to protect your skin from _____ sun.   A B C D

   (A) a   (C) the
   (B) an   (D) Ø

9. Hannah doesn't eat _____ spaghetti.   A B C D

   (A) much   **(C)** the
   (B) many   **(D)** a few

10. —What does Ethan do?   A B C D
    —He's _____ accountant.

   (A) a   **(C)** the
   (B) an   **(D)** Ø

11. Can you turn on _____ TV? I want to watch the news.   A B C D

   (A) a   **(C)** the
   (B) an   **(D)** Ø

12. —I rented _____ DVD last night.   A B C D
    —Oh? Which one?

   (A) a   **(C)** the
   (B) an   **(D)** Ø

PART TWO

Each sentence has four underlined words or phrases. The four underlined parts of the sentence are marked A, B, C, and D. Circle the letter of the <u>one</u> underlined word or phrase that is NOT CORRECT.

Example
Ana <u>rarely</u> <u>is drinking</u> coffee, but <u>this morning</u> she <u>is having</u> a cup.   A Ⓑ C D
      A   B   C   D

13. <u>The</u> news <u>were</u> very sad, and everyone <u>was</u> talking about <u>it</u>.   A B C D
    A   B   C   D

14. Melissa <u>has</u> been <u>a</u> honor student ever since she began her <u>studies</u> at   A B C D
         A   B   C

   <u>the university</u>.
      D

15. I need <u>some advice</u> about what to bring to my <u>aunt's</u> house on   A B C D
        A   B

   <u>new year's eve</u> next <u>Thursday</u>.
     C   D

16. How <u>many</u> times do I have to tell you not to leave <u>your</u> wet <u>shoes</u>   A B C D
       A   B   C

   on <u>a</u> kitchen floor?
      D

17. Mathematics <u>are</u> Allison's favorite school <u>subject</u>, and she always <u>gets</u> high   A B C D
            A   B   C

   grades.
    D

18. I have <u>a little</u> money, so I can't take <u>a</u> vacation until <u>next</u> year at <u>the</u> earliest.   A B C D
       A   B   C   D

19. We need to pick up <u>some sugar</u> and <u>banana</u> at <u>the</u> supermarket on <u>the</u> way   A B C D
                  A   B   C   D

   home.

20. Erin turned on <u>the</u> TV in order to see <u>the</u> weather report on <u>an</u> evening <u>news</u>.   A B C D
          A   B   C   D

Test: Units 23–26

PART ONE

Circle the letter of the correct answer to complete each sentence.

Example
Jason never _____ coffee.   A Ⓑ C D

(A) drink   (C) is drinking
(B) drinks   (D) was drinking

1. I have _____ boss in the world.   A B C D

   (A) a good   (C) the best
   (B) best   (D) the better

2. Jessica is an excellent employee. She works _____, and she's   A B C D
   very dependable.

   (A) as hard   (C) harder than
   (B) hard   (D) hardly

3. The apple pie smells _____.   A B C D

   (A) more wonderfully   (C) wonderful
   (B) the most wonderfully (D) wonderfully

4. The larger the apartment, the _____ the rent.   A B C D

   (A) expensive   (C) more expensive
   (B) expensively   (D) most expensive

5. That's _____ story I have ever heard.   A B C D

   (A) a ridiculous   (C) the more ridiculous
   (B) the ridiculous   (D) the most ridiculous

6. This living room isn't as _____ ours.   A B C D

   (A) big as   (C) bigger than
   (B) bigger   (D) biggest

7. Alexis drives more _____ Kyle.   A B C D

   (A) careful as   (C) careful than
   (B) carefully as   (D) carefully than

8. Is there anything else on TV? This show doesn't seem _____. A B C D

   (A) interested   (C) interestingly
   (B) interesting   (D) more interested

9. Riding in a car is more dangerous _____ flying. A B C D

   (A) as   (C) than
   (B) from   (D) that

10. Please call if you're going to arrive _____. A B C D

    (A) as late   (C) lately
    (B) late   (D) later than

11. It's getting more and _____ to find a cheap apartment. A B C D

    (A) difficult   (C) more difficult
    (B) less difficult   (D) more difficult than

12. She plays the piano _____ as she sings. A B C D

    (A) as beautiful   (C) more beautifully
    (B) as beautifully   (D) the most beautifully

PART TWO

Each sentence has four underlined words or phrases. The four underlined parts of the sentence are marked A, B, C, and D. Circle the letter of the <u>one</u> underlined word or phrase that is NOT CORRECT.

Example
Ana <u>rarely</u> <u>is drinking</u> coffee, but <u>this morning</u> she <u>is having</u> a cup. A Ⓑ C D
     A   B   C   D

13. Today will be <u>colder</u>, <u>wetter</u>, and <u>windier</u> <u>that</u> yesterday. A B C D
               A   B   C   D

14. This <u>nice</u> <u>new</u> apartment looks <u>perfectly</u> for a <u>young</u> couple. A B C D
     A B   C   D

15. Our <u>new</u> printer doesn't operate as <u>quiet</u> <u>as</u> our <u>old</u> one. A B C D
     A   B C   D

16. The clothes at Brooks are <u>nicer</u>, <u>interesting</u>, and <u>less expensive</u> <u>than</u> A B C D
                   A   B   C   D

    the clothes at B & S Department Store.

17. This is the <u>more interesting</u> and the <u>funniest</u> book I have <u>ever</u> <u>read</u>. A B C D
          A   B   C D

18. Thompson controlled the ball <u>the best</u>, kicked the ball <u>the farthest</u>, and A B C D
                   A   B

    ran the <u>faster</u> <u>of</u> all the players.
       C D

19. The critic was <u>amused</u> by the <u>funny</u> story line, but she found the acting A B C D
          A   B

    <u>extremely</u> <u>unexcited</u>.
   C   D

20. It's getting <u>easy</u> and <u>easier</u> to find a <u>good</u>, <u>inexpensive</u> digital camera. A B C D
         A   B   C   D

Test: Units 27–32

PART ONE

Circle the letter of the correct answer to complete each sentence.

Example
Jason never _____ coffee.   A Ⓑ C D

(**A**) drink   (**C**) is drinking
(**B**) drinks   (**D**) was drinking

1. Do you enjoy _____?   A B C D

(**A**) swim   (**C**) the swimming
(**B**) swimming   (**D**) to swim

2. I'm looking forward to _____ on vacation.   A B C D

(**A**) be going   (**C**) going
(**B**) go   (**D**) have gone

3. The doctor advised Dylan to stop _____.   A B C D

(**A**) for smoking   (**C**) smoking
(**B**) smoke   (**D**) to smoke

4. She's exercising more in order _____ weight.   A B C D

(**A**) for not gaining   (**C**) not to gain
(**B**) not for gaining   (**D**) to gain not

5. I'm excited _____ starting my new job.   A B C D

(**A**) about   (**C**) of
(**B**) for   (**D**) to

6. Maria is not used to _____ alone.   A B C D

(**A**) live   (**C**) lived
(**B**) lives   (**D**) living

7. Have you ever considered _____ jobs?   A B C D

(**A**) change   (**C**) changing
(**B**) changed   (**D**) to change

8. Where did he use to _____?   A B C D

(**A**) live   (**C**) lives
(**B**) lived   (**D**) living

9. Jasmine is interested _____ to college.　　　　　　　　　　A B C D

　(A) for going　　　　　　(C) to go
　(B) in going　　　　　　(D) to going

PART TWO

Each sentence has four underlined words or phrases. The four underlined parts of the sentence are marked A, B, C, and D. Circle the letter of the one underlined word or phrase that is NOT CORRECT.

Example
Ana <u>rarely</u> <u>is drinking</u> coffee, but <u>this morning</u> she <u>is having</u> a cup.　　A Ⓑ C D
　　　A　　　B　　　　　　　　　　C　　　　D

10. <u>Collecting</u> <u>stamps</u> <u>are</u> <u>a</u> popular hobby.　　　　　　　　A B C D
　　　　A　　　　B　　C D

11. Cody needs a ladder because he's <u>not</u> <u>enough tall</u> <u>to</u> <u>reach</u> the shelf.　　A B C D
　　　　　　　　　　　　　　　　A　　B　　　C　D

12. When <u>do</u> you <u>expect</u> <u>him</u> <u>being</u> here?　　　　　　　　　A B C D
　　　　A　　　　B　　C　　D

13. <u>Before</u> <u>leaving</u> the office, please <u>remember</u> <u>locking</u> the door.　　A B C D
　　　A　　B　　　　　　　　　　　C　　　D

14. Olivia <u>enjoys</u> <u>dancing</u> and looks forward <u>to</u> <u>learn</u> the latest dances.　　A B C D
　　　　A　　B　　　　　　　　C　D

15. After <u>moving</u> to Canada, Gisela had to get <u>used</u> <u>to</u> <u>do</u> everything in English.　A B C D
　　　　A　　　　　　　　　　　　　B　　C　D

16. Alyssa was so excited <u>about</u> <u>winning</u> the contest that she <u>forgot</u> <u>meeting</u>　　A B C D
　　　　　　　　　　A　　B　　　　　　　　C　　D

　her husband at the restaurant.

17. Zach <u>didn't run</u> fast <u>enough</u> <u>for</u> <u>win</u> the race.　　　　　　A B C D
　　　　A　　　　　B　　C　D

18. Emily <u>avoids</u> <u>going</u> <u>to</u> parties because she has trouble <u>to remember</u> people's　A B C D
　　　　A　　B　C　　　　　　　　　　　　　　D

　names.

19. <u>To do</u> sit-ups <u>is</u> hard work, and many people don't <u>enjoy</u> <u>doing</u> them.　A B C D
　　A　　　　B　　　　　　　　　　　C　　D

20. Ryan's father forced <u>him</u> <u>to apologize</u> <u>of</u> <u>breaking</u> the window.　　A B C D
　　　　　　　　　A　　B　　　C　　D

Test: Units 33–37

PART ONE

Circle the letter of the correct answer to complete each sentence.

Example

Jason never _____ coffee.   A (B) C D

(A) drink   (C) is drinking
(B) drinks   (D) was drinking

1. According to the law, everyone must _____ a license in order to drive.   A B C D

   (A) has   (C) have to
   (B) have   (D) to have

2. _____ rain tomorrow?   A B C D

   (A) Is it going to   (C) Should it
   (B) May it   (D) Would it

3. I _____ arrive on time, so please start dinner without me.   A B C D

   (A) could   (C) may not
   (B) may   (D) should

4. Jamie prefers working at home _____ working in an office.   A B C D

   (A) more   (C) that
   (B) than   (D) to

5. You _____ forget to pay your taxes.   A B C D

   (A) don't have to   (C) must
   (B) have to   (D) must not

6. According to the weather forecast, there _____ some rain tomorrow.   A B C D

   (A) could   (C) may be
   (B) may   (D) maybe

7. It's dark out. It _____ be late.   A B C D

   (A) could   (C) must
   (B) might   (D) ought to

8. —Is Caleb an exchange student?
   —I'm not sure. He _____.   A B C D

   (A) could   (C) must not be
   (B) couldn't   (D) could be

9. When _____ you supposed to call James?   A B C D

   (A) do   (C) must
   (B) are   (D) should

10. You _____ buy a gift, but you can if you want to.   A B C D

    (A) have to   (C) must
    (B) don't have to   (D) must not

11. We _____ a new car, but we got a used one instead.   A B C D

    (A) are going to buy   (C) were going to buy
    (B) are buying   (D) were buying

12. —Do you think Warren is over 20?   A B C D
    —He _____ be. I've known him for more than 20 years!

    (A) could   (C) might
    (B) has to   (D) must not

13. —Are you going to the party tonight?   A B C D
    —I _____. I'm pretty tired.

    (A) could   (C) 'd prefer to
    (B) don't like to   (D) might not

PART TWO

Each sentence has four underlined words or phrases. The four underlined parts of the sentence are marked A, B, C, and D. Circle the letter of the <u>one</u> underlined word or phrase that is NOT CORRECT.

Example
Ana <u>rarely</u> <u>is drinking</u> coffee, but <u>this morning</u> she <u>is having</u> a cup.   A Ⓑ C D
      A   B   C   D

14. <u>I'd</u> rather <u>having</u> dinner at home <u>than</u> <u>eat</u> out.   A B C D
    A   B   C D

15. My sister <u>may</u> <u>arrives</u> before <u>I can</u> <u>get</u> to the train station.   A B C D
        A   B   C   D

16. Why <u>do</u> you <u>prefer</u> newspapers <u>than</u> magazines<u>?</u>   A B C D
       A   B   C   D

17. Jared <u>will be</u> <u>supposed</u> <u>to be</u> there tomorrow, but he <u>can't</u> go.   A B C D
          A   B   C   D

18. It <u>must</u> rain <u>tonight</u>, so I <u>prefer</u> <u>to stay</u> home.   A B C D
      A   B   C   D

19. You <u>don't have to</u> <u>drive</u> so fast or you <u>could</u> <u>get</u> a ticket.   A B C D
        A   B   C   D

20. Rachel <u>is going to take</u> the train, but she <u>decided</u> that she preferred <u>to drive</u>.   A B C D
        A   B   C   D

Answer Key for Tests

Note: Correct responses for Part Two questions appear in parentheses.

UNITS 1–8

Part One

1. B	10. A	19. D	28. A
2. C	11. D	20. C	29. A
3. A	12. B	21. B	30. C
4. B	13. A	22. B	31. D
5. C	14. B	23. C	32. B
6. B	15. A	24. D	33. D
7. A	16. A	25. A	34. B
8. D	17. A	26. D	35. C
9. B	18. B	27. A	36. D

Part Two

37. D (is taking OR is going to take)
38. D (wants)
39. D (like)
40. B (eats)
41. B (are you)
42. A (doesn't)
43. B (he rarely)
44. D (don't look)
45. A (always works)
46. D (feels)
47. C (is shining)
48. D (dropped)
49. A (was)
50. B (use to)
51. D (got)
52. C (got)
53. A (did you)
54. B (was driving)
55. A (gets)
56. D (will tell OR is going to tell)
57. C (I leave)
58. B (is going to be)
59. A (won't)
60. D (is going to have OR is having)

UNITS 9–10

Part One

1. B	4. A	7. C	10. A
2. B	5. B	8. B	11. D
3. D	6. D	9. D	

Part Two

12. A (it over)
13. D (me)
14. B (called)
15. D (you up)
16. C (yourself OR yourselves)
17. A (each other OR one another)
18. B (each other's)
19. D (myself)
20. D (pick up OR pick some stamps up)

UNITS 11–15

Part One

1. A	4. D	7. B	10. D
2. B	5. C	8. B	11. A
3. D	6. C	9. C	12. A

Part Two

13. A (will you)
14. D (?)
15. C (if)
16. C (have)
17. B (leave)
18. D (please *goes after* you, remember, *or* newspaper)
19. A (to be)
20. B (telling)

UNITS 16–20

Part One

1. B	5. D	9. C	13. B
2. B	6. C	10. B	14. D
3. D	7. D	11. B	
4. B	8. C	12. B	

Part Two

15. C (worked)
16. A (has)
17. A (rented)
18. D (got)
19. C (has had)
20. D (yet)

UNITS 21–22

Part One

1. C		7. D	
2. C		8. C	
3. B		9. A	
4. B		10. B	
5. A		11. C	
6. C		12. A	

Part Two

13. B (was)
14. B (an)
15. C (New Year's Eve)
16. D (the)
17. A (is)
18. A (little)
19. B (bananas)
20. C (the)

UNITS 23–26

Part One

1. C	7. D
2. B	8. B
3. C	9. C
4. C	10. B
5. D	11. C
6. A	12. B

Part Two

13. D (than)
14. C (perfect)
15. B (quietly)
16. B (more interesting)
17. A (most interesting)
18. C (fastest)
19. D (unexciting)
20. A (easier)

UNITS 27–32

Part One

1. B	6. D
2. C	7. C
3. C	8. A
4. C	9. B
5. A	

Part Two

10. C (is)
11. B (tall enough)
12. D (to be)
13. D (to lock)
14. D (learning)
15. D (doing)
16. D (to meet)
17. C (to)
18. D (remembering)
19. A (Doing)
20. C (for)

UNITS 33–37

Part One

1. B	8. D
2. A	9. B
3. C	10. B
4. D	11. C
5. D	12. B
6. C	13. D
7. C	

Part Two

14. B (have)
15. B (arrive)
16. C (to)
17. A (is OR was)
18. A (might OR may OR could)
19. A (must not OR 'd better not)
20. A (was)